D1569482

From Rattlesnakes to Road Agents

Aunt Fan at the age of seventy, ready for a party.

From Rattlesnakes to Road Agents

Rough Times on the Frio

By Frances Bramlette Farris

Edited with an Introduction by C. L. Sonnichsen

Number Three in the
CHISHOLM TRAIL SERIES

Texas Christian University Press / Fort Worth

Library of Congress Cataloging in Publication Data

Farris, Frances Bramlette, b. 1865.
  From rattlesnakes to road agents.

  (Chisholm Trail series; no. 3)
  1. Farris, Frances Bramlette, b. 1865.   2. Frio County
(Tex.)—Biography.   3. Frio County (Tex.)—Social life
and customs.   4. Ranch life—Texas—Frio County—History
—19th century.   I. Sonnichsen, C. L. (Charles Leland),
1901–   .   II. Title.   III. Series.
F392.F9F37   1985   976.4′44206′0924 [B]   84-2500
ISBN 0-912646-94-2
ISBN 0-87565-005-8 (pbk.)

Designed by
Whitehead & Whitehead / Austin

CONTENTS

From Rattlesnakes to Road Agents

INTRODUCTION

IN 1943, WHEN THIS BOOK was first thought of, Civil War and Reconstruction days, after seventy years, seemed legendary and remote. It was hard to believe that any of the hardy men who had come to Texas in covered wagons and fought the Comanches were still alive. They did turn up every now and then, however, along with the women who shared their lives. Frances Bramlette Cochran Farris—Aunt Fan to her friends and relatives—was one of those women. Born in 1865, she grew up among the brush pastures and cotton patches in Frio County, south of San Antonio, and knew first-hand the trials and perils of pioneer life, from rattlesnakes to road agents. She survived drouths and floods, Indian raids, neighborhood feuds, and some very hard times, but she had the pioneer's indomitable soul and enjoyed her life to the fullest. She meant it when she said, "Even the work was fun."

Her people were Southerners of good stock with great family pride—perhaps an important reason for their survival. They expected much from themselves, and they usually delivered. It was significant that when times were hard the women did their own washing—and hired a black woman to hang out the clothes so the fact would not be known. The important thing was that they did the washing.

These were the aspects of pioneer life that little Fan observed most closely and remembered best, seeing it all from a girl's point of view. She recalled what people ate and wore, what they did for fun, how girls made themselves pretty for a party, what kind of human beings they were and what sort of lives they led. By 1943 a good many reminiscent books about post-Civil War Texas were in the libraries. Aunt Fan read them and decided that her experiences were as interesting as anybody's. After all, Bigfoot Wallace, Texas' most famous scout and Indian fighter, immortalized in John C. Duval's biography, had lived with her family for thirty years and had finished his days in her own home. He was only one of many interesting people she had known. She began putting some of her memories down on paper and wondered if she could possibly make a book of them. By this time she was living in her final home in Coronado, California, but her cousin Sarah Thomas Maddox of El Paso, my student and friend, was in communication with her and knew of her dream. She put us in touch with each other, and we began to exchange letters about the book. She sent me some of her pages; I thought they looked promising; and I agreed to try to put it all together for her. Late in 1943 the project got under way, and in September, 1944, the book was finished.

We soon found that it was early days for this sort of bread-and-butter narrative. The pulp westerns were going strong. Zane Grey was riding tall in the saddle. The mythical West was the only West most people knew or cared about; the reaction against western hokum had hardly begun; the interest in the West-that-really-was was in its infancy; and curiosity about the lives of women in the West was still farther away. Aunt Fan could have supplied the gory details that readers craved. She had seen the blood flow and the bodies on the ground—bodies of her friends and relatives—but like so many people of her generation, she did not choose to talk about these matters. She told a little about the terror and suffering of her people as the stealing and killing in a neighborhood feud went on but she would never name the families lined up against them. "I could give the names of every one of them," she said, "but all of them have children, grandchildren, and all kinds of relatives who I doubt ever have known that their forefathers were such men as they were. They are good citizens and in some cases have married into fine families, and I don't think I'd want to run the risk of getting them or myself into trouble."

When I asked her for details of another feud situation in the Frio country, she wrote

> "I am very sorry I can't remember very much about the Franks and Childress feud. My father was a friend of the Franks boys. Dan and Billie I think were their names. I remember Father took them food when they were in hiding from the law just after killing one of the other faction and Dan Franks having some beautiful buttons on his shirt and my sister and I (very small) admiring them, he would take us up on his lap and let us each cut a button off his cuffs. How proud we were of our beautiful buttons.

Obviously little Fan was more interested in buttons than in blood, a fact which did her no good with the editors who read her manuscript. It was unfortunate also, from the editorial point of view, that she was a Southern lady who used standard English and wrote well. She probably could have talked Texan, but she never did. Thus she had two strikes against her as a Texas author, and her book was never published. Her only literary achievement was publication by the *Southwest Review* (Winter 1944) of an essay titled "The Domestication of Bigfoot Wallace," based on one of her chapters.

Forty years later the climate had changed. The well was dry and the water had become precious; such chronicles as hers involving the life experiences of western women were being published and re-published. It was possible now to interest editors in Aunt Fan's simple annals—too late to make her happy.

Her recollections could be documented. The Texas papers were full of stories about the events of the seventies which she describes. The Indian raids of the spring, summer, and fall of 1870 brought anguished reports to the editors. The *San Antonio Herald* for April 23, 1870, for example, carried a story called "The Moon and the Indians":

On Saturday night last the Indians made their regular monthly raid into the settlements directly south of San Antonio. They appeared at different places on the same night, and although not in large numbers . . . there may have been many of them. . . . On the Chicon they killed several horses and drove away many more . . . they probably crossed the border near Laredo, into Mexico . . . .

On December 14 of that same year J. P. Dumas of "Dog-town, Rio Frio" complained to the *San Antonio Herald* that the Indians were at it again. On September 25 thirty horses had been run off at Alligator Lake. The band had murdered Thomas Stringfellow and his wife, wounded their daughter, and carried off two small boys. Moving on, they rounded up 195 more horses at various ranches and "crossed the river above Fort Clark unmolested." In utter gloom the writer commented: "This section will soon be depopulated, unless our law-makers demand reparation from the Mexican authorities . . . . Our troops seem also indifferent to our condition."

In 1878 the great drouth was under way. The *Western Chronicle* (Floresville) remarked that there was "no fun, no funds, no rain, no grass, no milk, no butter . . . water holes nearly all dried up, and the average citizen uses rather rough language . . . when he is compelled to draw water from a hundred-foot well to water a five-dollar horse."

The drouth was still on a year later. The *Chronicle* moaned on April 10, 1879, "Never was rain needed worse at this season of the year."

This was the way Aunt Fan remembered it.

Another of her stories is confirmed by the *Austin Daily Statesman* for August 19, 1874, quoting the *Waco Advance*:

A rumor has been going the rounds for several days that Bill Posey refused to work at the penitentiary, and was accordingly put into the tank with his feet tied down and the water turned on. Bill refused to pump it and was drowned. A day or so will show whether the report was true or not.

More corroboration would be easy to add, but documentation is hardly necessary. Aunt Fan's memory is her best and only source of information and what she reports is what she saw and was part of herself. She recounts what she alone could tell, and she does it with vigor and charm.

Her editor had only to go through her letters as they came in, assemble the material in chapters, add a comma here and there, and let her speak for herself.

She was a lively, loving, irrepressible, indomitable person, full of fun and mischief and at the same time proud and sensitive. At the end of her life she could still sing with enthusiasm, just as her mother did, "Oh, yes, I am a Southern girl."

She was ninety-three in 1958 when her health failed and her mind and memory with it, but her strong and tender spirit lives on in her reminiscences.

C. L. Sonnichsen

Louisa Thomas Bramlette, Fan's mother, in middle age.

KINFOLKS

In the South we like to know who a person's grand-father was, and I shall start by introducing mine. On my mother's side he was John Weathersby Thomas, who lived more than a hundred years ago on a plantation at Thomas-town, Mississippi, which was named for his family. His hobby was raising fine horses, and he had one mare which he thought was the best in the land. He matched her in several races and she surpassed his wildest dreams. Then the race of races was to be run. Grandfather was so sure of his mare's superiority that he staked his all on her—plantation, slaves, and furniture. Grandmother sat watching, and when the race was over, she fainted—the mare had lost.

Having nothing left but the mare, Grandfather sold her for a thousand dollars and bought wagon, wagon sheet, and a yoke of oxen with the money. Then he packed his personal effects, put his family and Aunt Jane (Grandmother's personal maid) into the wagon, and started off for Texas.

While crossing the Mississippi on the ferry, one of the oxen became too eager to be on his way and stepped off into the river. Grandfather said, "If he sinks, our destiny is here; if he swims, we go on to Texas." To the amazement of all, he swam. When the ferry reached the other side, they captured him, hitched him to the wagon again, and started off across the prairie toward Texas.

They made one crop in Louisiana, made another just across the Red River in Texas, moved on to Hays County, to Lockhart in Caldwell County, to Blanco County finally, where they arrived in 1841, when my mother was eight years old. It had taken them since 1838 to come that far. Mother said that when the autumn leaves began to fall Grandfather Thomas pulled stakes and moved always west.

Evidently Grandmother Thomas did not adjust so well to pioneering, because the older girls had to assume family responsibility at a very early age. She died after the birth of her eighth child, and then Mother took charge of the home and family. Aunt Jane taught her and her sisters to spin, weave, sew, make beds, knit and crochet.

I don't know a great deal about my grandmother, but she brought many lovely dresses made of silk, lace, and velvet, and some jewelry and silver, from her home in Mississippi. Her name was Perlina Joslyn and her mother was a cousin of Robert E. Lee.

My mother had all the pioneering qualities that Grandmother lacked. She was not a powerful woman, being small and slender, but there was nothing weak about her. She had an expressive, firm mouth, and we could tell by the set of it what the answer to our entreaties would be. She had a rather slender, heart-shaped face, light brown eyes and hair, small but capable-looking hands, a creamy complexion, pink cheeks, and bright eyes.

One of her teachers near Lockhart was a Mr. Esterbrook who wrote many songs. In one he mentioned mother. I can only remember snatches of it, but it was something like this:

> Louisa in her quiet beauty always does her
> duty
> And practices the Golden Rule
> She mothers her sisters and her brothers
> And sends them all to school.

She had a sense of humor and enjoyed recreation, but with her, duty came before pleasure and she believed one should desist from pleasure if pleasure weakened one's devotion to duty. She used to say, "If you dance, you have to pay the fiddler." And she and we paid our debt to the fiddler in hard labor. The hardest work we ever did was after we had indulged in pleasure.

Like any pioneer mother, she was thrifty, industrious, and ingenious. Her favorite saying was, "Willful waste makes woeful want." She threatened us constantly with the poorhouse in which she said we would end up "as sure as shooting," and we had the greatest horror of "Over the Hills to the Poorhouse." We thought it must be the worst place on earth.

She loved music, danced beautifully, and could do several solo dances which we delighted to see, but she was never very much interested in clothes. She kept a Sunday dress and the go-with-its but never seemed to buy or make any others. At home in the mornings she wore a dark calico dress with an apron tied over it; in the afternoon a light calico made with a tight blouse and full skirt.

She wore her hair parted in the middle and made a knot in the back in which she put a tucking comb. She had several tucking combs and this style of hair dressing was very becoming to her.

She was a dyed-in-the-wool Southerner and violently patriotic. She sang "Oh, yes, I am a Southern Girl" with more feeling and meaning than I ever heard put into a song before or since. In her later years when she was making a trip to visit us at El Paso, there was a band on the train, and it struck up "Dixie." One of the passengers looked disgusted and said, "It seems to me that old tune has been worn out." Mother stood up and said, "Young man, that piece will never wear out, as long as the heart of a Southerner beats." Another man jumped up, threw off his coat, and said, "I'll prove it to you right now, if you like." The other was not interested enough to fight over it, so they quieted down.

When she was about sixty-five she was in the cowpen milking a cow that had just had a new calf. One of the dogs ran up barking, and in lunging at the dog the cow knocked Mother down and stepped on her, breaking her hip. It never mended, and she had to walk on a crutch from then on, but she could get around on her crutch and do more work than most people can on two good legs.

She died at the age of seventy-nine and was buried beside my father in Longview Cemetery at Bigfoot, Texas. A large number of Mexicans and Indians came to her funeral bringing bouquets of wild flowers. They called her *La Angel Blanca*, for she had taken the responsibility for four generations of them since coming to Frio County, seeing to it that they had food, clothing, and medicine in times of sickness or when work was slack.

My father, MacHenry Bramlette, was born and reared on Grandfather Bramlette's tobacco plantation near Lynchburg, Virginia. He started to college at Richmond, but later he and his brother, Thomas E. Bramlette, went to Lexington, Kentucky, to study law. When the war between the United States and Mexico broke out, he ran away from school at the age of eighteen to "fight for his rights."

At the close of the Mexican War he, like Ulysses, took the long way home, tarrying in Texas and the South. He finally returned to Kentucky, where his brother had settled and become so successful in his career as a lawyer that he was a nominee for the office of governor. The War between the States was brewing, and in Kentucky, needless to say, the election did not pass without incident. One of these incidents was Father, who resented certain aspersions made against his brother and reacted in the manner usual in that state.

It being entirely too warm for him in Kentucky at that time, he hurried to Grandfather's home where, in a family conclave, it was decided that the Texas climate would benefit both Mac's health and Tom's political aspirations. So with a carriage, two fine horses, his personal Negro servant, Hal, and a thousand dollars in cash, Father started off to Texas. Uncle Tom was elected governor and Father's intended victim did not die after all, but he was so happy in Texas that he never desired to return to the states farther east.

When the War between the States became a reality, he joined Davidson's Texas Battalion, which served with General Hood, and went off again to "fight for his rights." Toward the end of the war Walter Hyatt, a fellow officer with whom Father had become very friendly, lay mortally wounded and asked Father to take his sword, saddle, picture, and personal effects back to Blanco, Texas, to the young lady he had planned to marry. Father, having a leave, complied with his request, fell in love with the girl, and married her himself.

When the war was over, he and Mother moved near Somerset in Atascosa County, where I was born, and about a year later we moved to Frio County, still farther southwest and still deeper into the wilderness. Uncle John Thomas, one of Mother's brothers, went with us. Later he married Sarah Duck, daughter of the sheriff of Atascosa County.

And that set the stage for what I remember of pioneer life in Texas sixty or seventy years ago.

I sometimes think things haven't changed so much. Not very long ago my daughter and I were asked to help entertain a group of boys in the Army, Navy, and Marine Corps—all volunteers. I asked the master of ceremonies to see if there were any boys from Texas there, and if there were I would like to have them come to my table for refreshments. They started coming, and you'd have thought I was besieged by Hood's Texans. They were the finest bunch of youngsters anyone would want to see. I asked them why they were so anxious to go to war. "Why," they said, "to fight for our rights." I thought, "My land, won't we ever get over fighting for our rights? I've heard that expression all my life. I hope some day we get them."

NEW COUNTRY

It was about 1867, when I was only a year or so old, that my father and mother moved from Somerset, a little way south of San Antonio, to the wild and thinly settled country farther southwest in Frio County. They drove a few cattle and some horses, everybody taking turns herding the stock and driving the covered wagon. Our old Negro mammy, Jane, rode in the wagon to take care of my sister and me, both of us being small.

As soon as we arrived at our new farm, Father and Uncle Sam Thomas set about trying to find some means of building us a shelter in which to live until we could get material to put up a permanent house. They proceeded to cut down some oak trees and hew part of the bark off to flatten them some-what. In that way they managed to put together four walls around a space about twenty feet square. The next thing was to get some kind of door, it being next to impossible to get lumber to make one out of. Looking around, they discovered a cow hide they had staked and dried, and since this seemed to be the best bet, they brought it in, set it up against the door opening, and considered it a pretty good fit. They built up some bed scaffolds by cutting mesquite forks and putting one end in the ground leaving the fork up—then cutting straight limbs to put in the fork. They made slats out of more poles, cut the tall sage grass to lay on the slats, and then spread our mattresses on top of the grass. Really, it wasn't too bad a bed.

One night not long after we had got everything all set up we retired early as usual (we had to get all lights and fires out early so the Indians who came through almost every night wouldn't find the house and massacre the family as they had many others). We had just about got off to sleep when the two dogs we had started snarling and barking and awakened us all. Then all at once the cow hide door flew across the yard and in burst the dogs and four big lobo wolves (we called them "loavers") all tangled up together, snapping and snarling and rolling all over the floor. We children got as far back on our beds as we could and even tried to climb the wall while old Aunt Jane yelled bloody murder: "Marse Mac, Marse Mac, for God's sake do something. The beasts am goin' to murder us alive."

Jane was pretty safe. She was sleeping in the covered wagon parked up beside the cabin.

Finally Father and my Uncle Sam got hold of a couple of dry-goods boxes, pitched them over the lobos' heads, and pushed them out. The dogs had had enough and crawled under the beds; and after Father got us children settled down and Jane stopped yelping, we finally got back to sleep again.

Poor old Aunt Jane seemed doomed to be destroyed by lobos. It was only a short time after the experience with the wolves and dogs that Jane got up early and went out to get wood to start the morning fire. She stayed and stayed until finally after about an hour Mother told Dad he had better get up and see about Jane, she had been gone so long. After she had persuaded him for some time, he decided it would be a good idea, so he went out, looked all around the cabin, and no Jane was to be found. So he started yelping "JANE!" as loud as he could, and after some time Jane says, "Here I is, Marse Mac, up in this tree, but don't look cause I'se got no clothes on. The wolves caught me and has tore every rag off. Go to the house, Marse Mac, and tell Miss Lou to come and bring me some clothes." And sure enough the poor old thing was scratched and bitten all over and every scrap of clothing torn off her. Besides being hurt she was in an awful rage. She said, "Miss Lou, I don't know why you don't take these little childs and go back to your good old pappy. I don't know what for you want to follow Marse Mac out to this heathen country for, anyhow. We'se all goin' to be killed before we can get away."

A family from some place on the Frio River often came

by and stopped at our house. They had an old Negro mammy who had been scalped by the Indians and left for dead. The poor old wretch was found and taken care of by the family she lived with, and her head was such a terrible sight that we children were horror-stricken and would always hope if the Indians got us they would kill us before they scalped us. It seemed the country was so hard on the Negroes, with both wolves and Indians, that our old Mammy Jane said she'd "done made up her mind it was no place for the cullud folks." So she persuaded Mother to send her back to where she came from.

We soon found that we had to count rattlesnakes among our worst enemies. They seemed to bed up with the large rats that infested the country. Wherever you found a great mound of sticks, prickly pear, and anything else the animals could carry, with a huge hole underneath, you could be pretty sure to find both rats and rattlers there. The dogs were always hunting out the rats and scratching into their holes, and many of our good dogs were bitten and killed by the snakes which had bedded in with the rats.

When we heard the dog yelp, we knew he had been bitten. We could sometimes save him by cauterizing the wound and pouring grease down his throat, but he more often died than not.

The rattlers also lived in hollow trees, when the hollow was near the ground, and we children were in great danger when we ran our hands into those hollows to get rabbits out. They always took refuge in such places to get away from the dogs, and when they did we would get a long live-oak switch, stick it into the hollow until we were sure it touched the rabbit, turn and twist until it took hold of the fur and hide of the rabbit, and then pull him out, screeching and hollering. When we had got him out, the dogs would go away, thoroughly satisfied, and start chasing another one. Our parents always cautioned us never to stick our hands into the hollows until we were sure there were no snakes inside, but we often heard them rattling at the dogs, and sometimes they bit the rabbits when they ran inside. As luck would have it, not one of us children was ever bitten.

Others were not so lucky. One morning bright and early we heard someone outside the house calling, "Mestro! Mestro! Mestro Bramlette!" Father got out of bed and went to the door. It was one of our Mexicans who lived not far from our house. He said, "Come quick! My little boy is snake-bitten." So Dad and Mother got all the remedies together (they always kept a supply just in case) and followed the Mexican to where he was living in a little house at the edge of a chaparral thicket. They found the poor little fellow writhing and crying in terrible agony, his leg already swollen to twice its natural size. He had got up and gone outside when he heard his dog crying. A snake had bitten the dog, and when the boy went outside, he stepped on it and was bitten too. A rattler generally crawls away as soon as it strikes something, but this one had different ideas.

Father and Mother stayed all day trying all their remedies. Towards night the little fellow fell asleep. A little later the swelling began going down, and they knew he would live.

While we lived in the shack, which we added to from time to time to give us more room, my Uncle Sam Thomas was busy hauling logs for the new house we were some day to live in. Before long my uncle by marriage, Wynn Haynes, came out with Mother's sister Aunt Sarah to help tame the West. While he was with us Uncle Wynn helped to hew the logs and split shingles from the oak trees, of which there was an abundance. Uncle Wynn was very handy about the place and seemed able to do almost anything he put his hand to. I remember his making saddle trees of hickory wood and covering them with cow hide which he had tanned. They really made quite nice saddles. All the frontiersmen had to turn to something for their support. I can remember Mother making cheese and selling butter to help out.

When Mother came west she brought her old spinning wheel with her—the one she had used during the War between the States to make clothing for the family as well as for the boys who wore the gray. She never found much use for it after she arrived at her final home since she was unable to get cotton to spin her thread. When she had the opportunity, she traded the wheel for a fine, large female pig which soon brought nine more little pigs and so started a nice little stock of hogs.

We made something out of every scrap of anything we could get. Our remedies were made of wild herbs. We made yeast for our bread. We manufactured our own furniture, mattresses, quilts, bedspreads, curtains, and braided rugs. We raised geese for feathers, manufactured our own clothing, and found a good deal of our food growing wild.

It is surprising how many of the wild plants were good to eat. One of them was poke greens, which came up very early in the spring and tasted quite delicious. We parboiled them until tender and then transferred them to a frying pan of hot bacon grease. Just before taking them off the stove, we broke several eggs into the pan and stirred them up together. Poke salad was good too—every old frontiersman knows about poke salad. The plant grew under trees in the shade, and in fence corners, along with another plant that was good for greens called lamb's quarter. Mixed with wild mustard and boiled with salt pork the lamb's quarter wasn't hard to take either.

Something else which grew wild and was very plentiful was the mustang grape. These grapes were not so very good to eat raw but they made excellent jelly and preserves. The housewives were always glad when it was time for the mustang grapes to come in, for we had very little fruit. Even before they were ripe we began using them, for the green grapes before the seeds began hardening made wonderful green-grape pies. We children always enjoyed grape-gathering time for we were allowed to scale the trees and gather the fruit for our elders.

Then too there was a most delicious cactus fruit called a *petahaya* which grew on the rocky hills. The *petahayas* began ripening in early June in what seemed the very hottest weather. How we loved to roam over those rocky slopes and pick them. They were about the size of a small hen's egg and were literally covered with thorns, but when they were ripe we would each take a mesquite stick, touch the ripe ones, and the thorns would scatter in all directions, leaving fruit looking like a very small pineapple. And were they delicious! I think they had the best flavor of any fruit I ever ate. We would stay out on those hot, bare hills until we had filled all our buckets, even if it took all day; and when we finally got home, what a feast we had. We would put them in a bowl, pour cream and sugar over them, and oh, my! How delicious! We usually brought back enough for several days and felt amply repaid for all our walking in the heat gathering them.

I must tell you also about the grand wine the men folks made of the mustang grape, the best I think I ever drank. We had some German people living near us who were famous for making grape wine. Our folks gathered grapes for the two families and the Germans made the wine, at least a barrel for each. Of course our family could never use a barrel of wine, but we shared with all our friends, some of them living in town with no chance of making it for themselves. And even if they had lived in the country, they could never have made wine like those Germans.

Strange to say in those days you never saw a drunk person. My father having been reared mostly in Kentucky and Virginia, where most families kept liquor in their houses, always had his demijohn, and yet I never saw any of our men the least bit inebriated. My brother would never touch it, even when our parents gave it to us for colds.

Of course we could not live entirely on wild fruit and greens, and we grew our own vegetables—sweet potatoes by the ton and lots of pumpkins and kershaws. To save them through the winter we built great ricks of cornstalks. We would put mesquite forks in the ground and lay a long ridge pole in the forks. Then we would set corn stalks up against the ridge pole in the shape of the roof of a house until we had a thickness of perhaps twelve inches, and finish by stacking dirt against the corn, beginning at the bottom. When we were through we had a rick as long as we wanted it with walls at least a foot and a half thick. The next step was to begin piling the potatoes in so they would be next to the back of the rick, and as soon as we had enough to last the family through the winter we would start rolling in the pumpkins and kershaws at the front. When the time came to use them, we dug into the front for the pumpkins and into the back for potatoes, carefully covering up the openings with the stalks and dirt each time. In that way they never froze and we had the nicest, sweetest potatoes you ever ate, lasting well into the spring. The pumpkins also mellowed and sweetened in their winter den.

And then we made a lot of sorghum molasses. Uncle John Thomas bought a sorghum mill from someone near Somerset and had the man from whom he bought it come out and give him some instruction in running it. Then Uncle John advised all those who wanted sorghum molasses to plant a certain kind of sugar cane. When the time came, the growers were told to strip the leaves off their cane in the patch, cut the long, bare stalks, and haul them to the mill. He had a big response to his request for cane, for everybody was curious to know how his experiment would turn out. By the day set for the start of the procedure, several tons had been brought in and stacked, ready to go.

In the meantime Uncle John had been training his old dun horse Celum to pull the crank which turned the mill and ground out the juice of the cane. Old Celum had become so well trained that he didn't even require a driver but just started going around and around, stopping only when Uncle John would say, "Whoa, Celum!" But imagine Uncle John's horror after about five days of grinding when he went out to hitch Celum up and found his face swollen terribly—a rattler had bitten him. He tried every remedy he could think of and finally called Father, who seemed to be a jack of all trades, even unto veterinary surgery. Still Celum seemed to grow worse and worse. And when every snake-bite remedy known to frontiersmen had failed, Uncle said, "Mac, I've heard that if you read a certain chapter in the Bible and have faith, the animal will recover." Uncle John, being a good Christian, always seemed to have faith.

Father said, "John, that's all foolishness, but if you want to try it, why all right."

So Uncle John went to the house and brought out the Bible, and Father volunteered to hold Celum's head while Uncle John read. I'm sorry I've forgotten what chapter it was. It didn't seem to make any difference; old Celum died anyway.

Uncle John was hard put to it to find another horse to take Celum's place and kept having trouble. One day he remarked to some of the fellows who were always gathered round the sorghum mill that he was going to get another horse—the one he had now was so lazy and slow he would never get through with his molasses making. A hare-lipped fellow named Bill Nixon said, "John, why don't you get that bay horse of yours? He looks like a pretty good horse."

Uncle John replied, "I'd surely like to have him, but he's been gone for two or three weeks. I've looked for him everywhere and haven't found hide nor hair of him."

"I saw him yesterday," Bill told him, "with some strange horses over at the back of the Bramlette pasture."

"I'd certainly like to get hold of him," said Uncle John, "but I haven't got a horse to ride right now that could catch him, and he's the kind of horse that will run if he thinks anybody wants to put a saddle on him."

Several of the men heard this conversation and were listening when Bill volunteered to come over early next morning, bringing a horse for Uncle John, so the two of them could go catch the horse.

About seven o'clock next morning Bill appeared at the designated place, leading a somewhat fiery horse for Uncle John to ride. They mounted and were soon on their way but had been gone only a short time when we looked out and saw Bill coming in as fast as his horse would carry him. Uncle John's horse was directly behind him, the horn knocked off the saddle and the horse frightened almost into fits. The whole family rushed out to Bill. He looked like a statue glued to his saddle and had to be asked twice where on earth John was before he could answer.

When he could finally compose himself enough to reply, he groaned, "Oh, Lord! the Indians have got him—the Indians have got him!"

"Where?" asked Father.

"I don't know!"

"You must have some idea. Tell us about where."

"Over there where we were looking for the horse."

"Did they kill him?"

"Oh, I don't know! The last I saw of him he was crawling in a run on his all-fours into a thicket."

"But Bill, did the Indians shoot him off his horse, and how many Indians were there?"

"I don't know. I didn't look but a minute, and I don't *think* John looked that long."

It developed, when we finally got to the bottom of it, that three Indians with faces and bodies painted red and with red kerchiefs tied over their heads, stripped to the waist, had attacked them. They had charged in, shooting their pistols off and yelling the Indian yell. When Uncle John and Bill saw them coming, they started hightailing it for a nearby thicket. John's horse ran under a mesquite limb which wasn't high enough to miss the saddle, so John and the saddle horn were lost in transit.

Before enough men could be gathered to go after the Indians, Uncle John came staggering in, all bloody from his encounter with the overhanging limb and from crawling on his hands and knees into the thicket through brush and thorns. He was still very much upset and declared there must have been a dozen Indians after them, but he "was smart enough to outsmart them."

About that time in rode the Indians in the persons of Billy Winters, Doc Wilkins, and Bill Owens. They had heard the plan about going to catch Uncle John's horse and decided to play a prank. And were Uncle John and Bill Nixon mad! I thought we were going to have a shooting match over it before they got cooled off and could take it as a joke. For years afterward if you wanted to raise Uncle's ire you had only to mention the dozen Indians that chased him and Bill Nixon.

The three "Indians" caught the horse for Uncle John, so the episode ended and Uncle John finished his molasses making for that season with no more trouble. Almost all the neighbors had a nice supply, and besides being useful for food, the molasses afforded a lot of entertainment for the youngsters at their candy pullings. It made very nice candy. The pulling turned it a light yellow, almost white, and everyone was very fond of it.

It took some time, of course, for all this to happen. When we first moved to the new country Uncle Wynn Haynes supplied our sweetening by hunting bees, which were quite plentiful. He kept both his and our household well supplied with honey, besides taking a lot to market.

He also hunted deer. I shall never forget one occasion when Uncle Wynn started out after venison. We were getting scarce on fresh meat, so he started out with his big bay horse which, for some reason, he always called Skinny. Skinny could never be broken of shying at everything he saw when somebody was riding him. A piece of paper blown up by the wind would set him wild. When Uncle Wynn had killed his deer and got it tied on behind his saddle, Skinny happened to spy it. He began pitching and snorting, jerked away from Uncle Wynn, and managed to dislodge his load. With the carcass dragging at the end of the rope he came tearing down the road, the dust flying; and when we saw the horse come dragging something, we thought the Indians had killed Uncle Wynn and tied him to the rope, and that the horse was dragging him in. Even when we found that it was not our uncle on the end of the rope, we still thought the Indians had got him. Father and Uncle Sam saddled their horses and set out to look for him, but hadn't got far when they met Uncle Wynn coming in.

We didn't have much to do with in those days. There were no electric lights—it was some time before even coal oil lamps were in use. I remember seeing Mother twist a wick from a string off an undershirt and put it into a flat tin cup of lard. When she lit one end of the string, it would make a fairly good light. Later on Father found some funny-looking iron lamps which could be hung on the wall. They were supposed to burn grease, but used "sto' bought" wicks. We were very proud of them and used them until finally, some years later, we could get kerosene lamps.

I can remember when Father found the first ones on the market and brought three or four home from San Antonio along with a can of kerosene to use as fuel. They were made of shiny brass and seemed to us the prettiest things we ever saw. We immediately put our Negro maid Ann (who came to us after Mammy Jane left us) to work filling the lamps, putting wicks in, and getting them ready to light.

Unfortunately, when Ann tried to light one it exploded and cut her nose off. We really had some excitement then— blood streaming and children screaming until Father, who was pretty adept at surgical dressings, stuck her nose back on and with cotton and linen strips somehow managed to leave her with a fairly respectable nose. She had only a small scar to remind her of the incident.

After that we were quite wary about trying to light those lamps. It seems to me now that kerosene must have been much more explosive in those days.

Ann didn't hold her bad luck against us. She stayed with the family a long time. When she finally married a colored photographer and moved away from us, she had what she called her "white folks' room" in the house Alex built for her and we often stopped and spent the night in it. Her beds were white as snow and everything shone in her white folks' room, and her dining room was spotless with white tablecloth and all the things that the white folks were accustomed to having. Not a "nigger" appeared in sight while we were at the table— only Ann, who served us. When I was last in that part of the country, Ann and Alex Banks were still living in the same place, good and respectable people with a nice family.

But to get back to our housekeeping arrangements. Before we got our first stove, we had our kitchen built at the back of the house under a separate roof. Because Mother had hopes of getting a cookstove and didn't want to get the kitchen roof smoked up by cooking inside on the fireplace, she had Father and Henry Leuthy build her a rock fireplace just outside the kitchen. We used the kitchen at that time as a dining room.

The outdoor fireplace was built something on the order

of today's barbecue pits. All four sides were first built up to a height of about four feet—just right to stand up by comfortably—and on top of the four walls was one of those large sheet rocks cut just to fit. Then three sides were built up about three feet farther to keep the wind from blowing the fire out. Before starting to cook, they would build up a good fire and wait till it had burned down to coals, then drag some of the live coals out onto the hearth and put the dutch skillet on them. The skillet lid they placed on top of the fire to heat, and while the skillet and lid were heating Mother would make up her biscuits, corn bread, or anything she wanted to cook. As soon as the skillet was hot, she would grease it, put in whatever she was cooking, and then take the long iron hook they always had for the purpose and put the lid on the skillet. This done, she would shovel some red-hot coals on top of the lid and everything was ready. Boy, that was the best bread anyone ever ate; and not only bread!—she would cook sweet potatoes, beef or pork roast, and practically anything else she wanted. At times there would be two or three dutch ovens on at the same time.

For the kettles and pots there was an iron rod across the top of the fireplace. We hung utensils on it to take care of the boiling and stewing, and though it wasn't as convenient as cooking on the stove, still I think the food had a far better flavor.

This cooking place was built just outside the kitchen proper under a large and shady liveoak tree, and the men built a sort of shed roof over it with a canvas to let down in front in case of rain. We used it for several months before Mother got her first stove. Then we moved our cooking into the big log kitchen, which, incidentally was useful for more reasons than one. The logs were made of the hardest hickory, which an ordinary bullet could not pierce, and it afforded us great protection later.

It must have been about this time that Father bought us a Wheeler and Wilson sewing machine. I remember distinctly the day the sewing-machine agent came to the house with that wonderful machine and gave us a demonstration, showing what beautiful ruffles it could gather, what lovely small tucks it could make, and what a remarkable quilter it had with which our sunbonnets could be quilted so easily. We paid a hundred dollars cash for it.

Mother's eyes were very bad at the time and we children were still too small to pedal a sewing machine, so Father decided he would take over. He thought it would be great fun to sew with a machine, and consequently it was he who took the instructions. I still think this was a little strange, for Father was never interested in any kind of manual labor, having been brought up in a Southern family who thought it a disgrace to work with the hands. Anyway he got a lot of kick out of running the machine.

As soon as our neighbors found out we had it, they began filing in with sewing to do. Josephine Gardner came several miles and brought her whole wedding trousseau. Father did a fine job until the novelty wore off, and then the machine sat around unused until my sister and I became large enough to run it.

Little by little we added to our comforts, and one day our new house was ready for occupancy. We were very proud of it, for it was the only house in that sparsely settled community that boasted a real plank floor and had so many rooms. There was a very large main room twenty by thirty feet, a front porch, a small room cut off the porch at one end, a shed room across the entire back, and the kitchen twenty feet from the rear of the house.

The walls were at first made of oak slabs or pickets, but a little later Father got lumber from San Antonio and had planks put in in place of the slabs. We were feeling very fine over having the first lumber house in the community when our happiness was interrupted by the death of one of the men who lived near us. It was a four-day trip to San Antonio and back, and the family was hard put to it to find some means of providing a coffin, so Father settled the difficulty by bringing a few of the men back with him and knocking some of the new planks out of our house to make one. It was winter time, and I'm telling you it was pretty cold in that house before we could get more lumber. We children put up a great kick about their tearing our house down, but Father shamed us when we got too loud.

We had the scare of our lives just before we moved into that house. My little brother Pat was just old enough to toddle around, and one day he escaped Mother's watchful eye and crawled out to the famous Bramlette well that furnished drinking water to people for miles around. It had a cover made of lumber—two doors, each about three feet wide, which closed together. Some one had left the doors unclosed and my little brother climbed up and seated himself on the curb, hanging his feet out over the open well. About that time our big old dog Sultan spied him, grabbed him by the skirt of his little pink calico dress, and began making an awful growling noise which attracted the attention of Mother. She ran to the well, frightened stiff, and rescued the baby. Sultan was pulling one way and Pat the other, and I shudder still to think that if that little pink slip had given way, he would have gone down sixty feet into twenty feet of water. Poor old Sultan had fallen into it before and had to be dragged out by a rope around his neck, which explains why he realized the danger when he saw the baby sitting on the well curb.

Sultan was one of the dogs who had participated in the fights with lobo wolves when we first moved into our cabin and had to use a cow hide for a door. He was very strong and a real cowboy. When any of us happened to be trying to pen a contrary steer or cow which insisted on going in the opposite direction from the one required, all we had to do was call Sultan. He would make one lunge, catch the animal by the nose, run between its fore legs, and turn it a complete somersault every time. When he let it go, it was a conquered animal and perfectly willing to be corraled. However, poor Sultan caught one too many. We had a massive and short-tempered old bull who once refused to be put into the pen and Sultan, trying to do his duty to the last, made his lunge, caught the bull's nose, and then failed to get out of the way in time. The bull fell on him and crushed him to death. We children set some sort of record for bawling and squalling when we heard of it.

MID PLEASURES AND POLITICS

A<small>FTER WE MOVED</small> into our new house, the fun really began. Since ours was the only plank floor in the vicinity, we were the logical people to give all the dances, and we had a great many. Though I was very young when all this started, I can remember Father always meeting the men at the door and asking them politely to turn in their arms until the dance was over. He took the rifle and one or two pistols which every man carried and locked them up in his old-fashioned oak desk, in that way avoiding what might have ended in killings as the two factions of which I'll tell you later always insisted on going to any and all kinds of entertainments.

When the word went out that there was going to be a *baile* at Bramlettes', people began gathering by dozens from early in the day the dance was to be given until after nightfall. People came from Friotown, from Pleasanton, from Benton, from even as far as San Antonio—in farm wagons, in buggies, in hacks, on horseback. You would have thought one of those famous old-time Baptist camp meetings was in progress, and when Jim Sadler and the two Halsey boys tuned up their fiddles and started the music rolling, everybody was ready to "cut it." And it went on until far into the next day.

I remember one young girl, just beginning to think she had reached the young lady stage, who had long yellow curls reaching below her waist. The house, which was built of pickets, was still not quite finished, the battens not having been put over the cracks. So some of the devilish boys got outside and pulled one of her curls through a crack with a switch and tied a stick to it. Then they came inside to watch Tina try to get up when she went to dance. The young men were somewhat disappointed when she discovered what they had done and got help in extricating herself.

The mornings after the dances, I remember my parents always prepared breakfast for the folks to eat before leaving. All the women would get busy in the combination kitchen and dining room, where there was always plenty of flour, milk, eggs, butter, and fresh-killed meat. It would, of course, take quite a while to cook enough to feed the crowd, but by mid-afternoon they would all be on their way home.

We also entertained politicians. Our place was about half way between Pleasanton and Friotown, the county seat, and during election years we always had plenty of company—candidates for all the state offices from governor down, and all the county officers too. They found it very convenient to stop over for a night and feel out their chances for election; perhaps they might even spend a week discussing pros and cons and trying to get Father to electioneer for them. When Father thought the right man was a candidate for the right place, he would put the proverbial jug in the little old green hack and be gone for a couple of weeks. He usually elected his man. Before our Uncle Wynn Haynes got into office, Dad had had an eye on him for some time. Uncle Wynn understood surveying and had his compass and other paraphernalia so Father approached him with the idea of running for county surveyor. Like all Father's in-laws he protested that he couldn't hold the office—didn't know one thing about it to start with. Father convinced him that he could hold it, and with Father's promise to help him out, he finally decided to try it. He was elected and held the office for twenty-five or thirty years.

Father also managed political campaigns for Uncle John Thomas, who held the office of justice of the peace for many years and then became county judge. Aunt Sarah Thomas had a lot of confidence in Father, but she was always a little fluttery at such times. She had a little slide window in her kitchen facing the road, and I don't think a person ever passed without her seeing him and wanting to know what he was up to. On election day that window was never unoccupied. She would exclaim, "Now I wish you'd just look! There goes a whole wagon load of the Joneses. I'll just bet they are going to vote against John!"

The night before the election she would send one of the boys over to get "Mac" (my father) to spend the night, fearing he wouldn't be out in time in the morning. Father would always say, "Sarah, I can't electioneer without a bottle of electioneering whiskey."

She would reply, "Now Mac, I've got a bottle in there but don't you go drinking any of it until after the election." Then she would peep through the window and say, "Come here quick, Mac. There goes Mr. Davis with a whole load of Mexicans. I just know he's going to vote them against John. You'd better hurry on down there and see what's going on."

"But Sarah," Dad would say, "the polls don't open until seven o'clock."

"I don't care if they don't! You *ought* to be there anyway."

She was always nervous until she found out that Uncle John was elected.

Sometimes I think we had more fun in those days, though our pleasures were simple. We all sang a good deal. I don't remember a one that had a good voice, but all joined in from the oldest to the youngest and did their best. There were hunting and fishing trips to the Medina, Frio, Hondo, and Guadalupe rivers. At home we played many games together. On moonlight nights we played them outside.

And as far as we were from civilization, we used our minds. We took *Godey's Ladies' Book* and any other publication we could get on homemaking. The men discussed religion, philosophy, and politics. Dad and Uncle Wynn Haynes even made a hobby of working problems in calculus. People sent them problems from far and near which they worked by the score, and they would argue for days over them.

Sometimes even the work was fun, for instance, washing clothes. The Bramlette pond (so called because Father owned the land on which it was situated) was a wash place for most of the community. They would all decide on a certain wash day, and several families would congregate, believing there was safety in numbers.

The men had made a bench of a split oak tree with the top side hewn off and planed smooth. On this the women placed the articles to be washed, especially the men's heavy shirts, jeans, trousers, and underwear, and pounded them with a paddle-shaped piece of wood made out of heavy lumber. The bench was called the battling bench and the paddle was known as the battling board. It seems as if they would have battled the clothes all to pieces, but that was the way they did it—just pounded to beat the band, sometimes calling in the men folks to help them battle.

Both men and women assisted at the community wash day. The men always brought their guns along to keep the Indians away while the women did the washing. They were also useful in lifting Father's kettle, which was the largest I ever saw—it took three men to lift it on the wagon. It stayed at the pond from one hog-killing time till the next (hog-killing time was generally in December or January).

Meeting at the pond was quite a social get-together as well as a time for work. The women lingered long after the washing operation was finished, discussing better ways to make preserves out of the wild fruit, make soap with "cracklins" after rendering the lard, and improve on other household arts.

Such incidents as the following amused us children. My Uncle John had an old ram he had raised from a lamb. Old Jerry they called him—and Old Jerry, though very docile with the family, didn't care much for strangers, particularly women. He would always follow the wagon when any of the family took off in it. If they managed to leave without his knowledge, he seemed to sense the way the wagon had gone and would follow. So he always showed up on wash days at the pond. The men had built a narrow platform out into the water for the women to use in dipping up water with their buckets. Once one of our neighbors, Mrs. Tilly, walked out on the platform with her bucket. We saw Jerry eyeing her from the rear and had an idea of what he might do. Mrs. Tilly took quite a little while in dipping up her water, and to our delight we saw Old Jerry make a straight rush for her. He took her kerwallop right in the rear, and she tumbled head-first into the pond, waist deep, while Jerry waited patiently on the bank to give her another whack. One of the men saw him and hauled him away amid shrieks of laughter from us children, saving poor Mrs. Tilly from further chagrin.

Another occasion on which everybody got together was a logrolling. I distinctly remember one I attended at an early age. We had two funny little Irishmen, Jimmy O'Grady and Pat King, who preempted a piece of land adjoining our place. They were well diggers and had dug most of the wells in that part of the country. In their spare time they grubbed up all the trees on the land they were preparing for cultivation and cut the logs in eight or ten-foot lengths. Then they invited all the neighbors to a logrolling. The women cooked up a regular dinner, each one bringing one or two things—meat, vegetables, cakes, pies, and so on. When we were all gathered at Jimmy's shack, the women went to making coffee and visiting while the men went out to roll the logs off the clearing, two or three men to a log. When all had been cleared off, they came in, tired but seemingly happy, to where the women had the big feed prepared. It didn't take Uncle Jimmy long after that to get in a nice field.

Now that I have mentioned Pat and Uncle Jimmy, I might as well tell what happened to them later. They dug their wells the hard way. They went at it with their picks and shovels in a hole about six feet in diameter, and had two men (sometimes only one) on top to draw up the dirt in boxes. On one occasion the man who drew the dirt up let the windlass slip in some way and the box went tumbling down at a terrific rate. Old Uncle Jimmy had a narrow escape from being crushed to death; and as it was, the box caught one of his legs and left him a cripple for life. That ended his well digging, but not his troubles. A final tragedy broke up his partnership with Pat. They were both very superstitious and one night when Pat's old red rooster crowed just before nine o'clock, they knew something was going to happen. "Pat," said Jimmy, "you know when a rooster crows before nine o'clock you are sure to hear of a death."

"And begad, Pat," said Jimmy, "I hope it's neither you nor I."

Two days later Pat went to the nearby town of Morse, got on a spree, and fell out of a second-story window, breaking his neck. Jimmy took vengeance by killing every rooster they had, thinking that would break the spell and prevent another rooster from crowing before nine o'clock.

Perhaps because of this precaution Uncle Jimmy lived to a ripe old age and, having neither kith nor kin, left his property to another Irishman named Pat Roach who moved into our settlement with his lovely family and was very kind to Jimmy in his old age.

To get back to our social gatherings, I must not forget to mention hog-killing time. Father always killed twenty-five to thirty fat hogs every year. He had to have two or three hired hands, for it was quite an undertaking and Dad was extremely averse to occupying himself with anything that smacked of manual labor. He never minded overseeing the work if it did not interfere with his afternoon siesta. When the hogs were killed, scalded, scraped, cut up, and reduced to hams, sausage, middlings, jowls, etc., we always managed to have enough left over to make what is known in West Texas as a son-of-a-bitch. This was a favorite dish which the family and the neighbors who were invited in to partake enjoyed immensely. I'm very sorry for folks who have never eaten this delicious concoction.

The one who often felt something missing from our frontier life was Father. The rest of us had never known the luxuries of the older states and didn't miss them, but it was different with Father. He was accustomed to having a Negro valet wait on him hand and foot and never did get used to the idea of not having a "lackey boy," which was the word for personal servant in his former vocabulary. He tried all sorts of boys, white, brown, red, and black, but none seemed to take the place of Hal, his former body servant. He could never boss the others around as he had bossed Hal. Then finally he came across an Indian boy who seemed promising. This one had been reared by the Mexicans and was known as Chink because his eyes resembled those of a Chinaman. Father called him Chinky-Chunky. He was very tractable for a few days. Father would ride up to the front of the house and call Chinky to take his horse, unsaddle, and feed him. Then perhaps Father would find he had left something out in the cow lot and would call on Chinky to go and get it. Then it was Chinky, bring me my pipe; Chinky, bring me a cup of coffee; and so on through the day. Chinky began to look more and more dejected, and finally things came to a climax when Father ordered Chinky to bring him the basin and towel to wash his feet (no bath tubs in those days). Right there Chinky rebelled. He hopped up and said, "Chinky-Chunky, Chinky-Chunky, all the time Chinky-Chunky. Goddam white man lazy too much!" Then he marched off the premises and that was the last we saw of him.

Yes, we had many things to enjoy and often found something to laugh about. I think of those days even while living here in the most beautiful city in the world with the loveliest friends one could wish for, and wonder if we were not better off then than now. In many ways I am sure we were—but we lived through some terrible experiences too.

Bigfoot Wallace's last home—where he was living when the Bramlettes took him in (Western History Collections, University of Oklahoma).

COMANCHE TROUBLE

ALONG WITH OUR OTHER TROUBLES we had Indians. The ones that infested our part of the country were Comanches, and they gave us some bad moments. I remember one time while we were still living in our first picket house we children (my sister, my little brother, who was born after our arrival, and I) persuaded my father to take us down to the branch. It was after a rain and we knew there would be water enough to go swimming. As we went along my little brother, who was riding on Father's back, said, "Look, look Pa, at the turkeys!" Father gave one glance and said, "Lie flat on your stomachs and don't speak or make any noise." It was Indians with feathers on their heads going down a path through the high sage grass, which came to their shoulders. Needless to say we were very still and not too disappointed when we didn't get our swim. When we were sure the Indians had had time to get some distance from us, we went back to the house, very grateful that we hadn't been scalped.

Bigfoot Wallace was living over on the Hondo when we first came to the country, but he spent a lot of time with us. He came down one day and told us how the Indians had shot and killed Mr. Galbreath's little boy, about twelve years old. His father had sent him out to unhobble one of the horses and bring him in to water, and when he stooped down to take the hobbles off, the Indians shot an arrow through him. Up to that time the Indians hadn't molested us much, but over on the Hondo they had made several raids, driving off horses and killing people. For a long time, what with wild animals, desperadoes and Indians, we never felt safe.

We had some relatives who lived between us and San Antonio at a little place called Benton City. One of the daughters had married a James Davis. The Davis family lived about thirty miles from us on the San Miguel and always made it to our house to spend the night when on their way to visit at Benton City. Once, on their way home from a visit, they stopped as usual and I thought it would be great fun to go home with them. We very seldom went anywhere and the prospect of a trip seemed very exciting, so my cousin Mary Davis joined me in persuading Mother to let me go. The Indians were really worse in that neck of the woods, and hardly a week passed that there was not a raid somewhere near. There were several large stock ranches around the Davis place and I suppose the Indians thought it a better place to find the horses they were generally after on their raids.

I stayed with my cousins about a week, frightened half to death all the time as news of depredations came in. Finally Mother, Father, and the other youngsters came to take me home, and, as the custom was in those days, remained several days. One night two nice young men, Max Franks and Frank Webb, stopped and asked my Cousin Jim if they could spend the night. He gladly complied with their request. After they had their breakfast next morning, they saddled their horses, one a fine, young newly broken bay horse, the other a tough Mexican cow pony. After thanking Cousin Jim, they started off, heading for some place on the Frio to bring in horses from a ranch belonging to one of them. About an hour or so after they had gone, we heard rapid shooting in the distance. I remember Mother saying, "Jim, what on earth do you suppose all that shooting is?" Cousin Jim replied that he thought it was the Perryman boys (neighboring ranchers) shooting wolves. "No," said Mother, "it's too regular and too much shooting for anyone killing wolves."

The shots seemed to come nearer, and the family began to think something bad was happening. After a time they all went out to the back of the house, in the direction of the firing, and as they stood there they saw Max Franks riding in. His poor horse was covered with sweat and could hardly stand—nose on the ground and every muscle quivering. The boy was white as a sheet and could hardly speak. Cousin Jim asked him what on earth was the matter, and when he could control his voice enough to reply, he said, "The Indians! They've killed Frank and followed me to within sight of the house."

He told how they were attacked by about fifty Indians and started back towards the ranch, the Indians shooting at them and they shooting back at the Indians. Frank, who was younger than he, started out as fast as the young horse could go. Seeing that he was leaving Max behind, he would wait for him to catch up. When Max could get close enough, he would tell the other to hold his horse back or it would give out on him, but the boy would get excited and turn loose as fast as he could go. Finally the young horse stopped and couldn't go any farther, so Max tried to get Frank to jump up behind him. He refused, saying, "No, if I do your horse can't carry us both and get back to the ranch. I'm done for anyway, and if we double on the horse we'll both be killed."

They got Max into the house, gave him something to drink, and finally got him somewhat calmed. Then Cousin Jim started calling his cowboys in and sending them to the outlying ranches to bring the men and families in to his ranch house where they usually gathered when there was danger of an attack by Indians. By nightfall there were about fifteen men (besides Cousin Jim's hired hands) there with their families, and late in the afternoon Cousin Jim delegated six of them to go out after the body of the young man who had been slain. They filled the bed of a large Studebaker wagon with hay, took plenty of ammunition, and, with the boy Max to show them the way, they set out.

They found the poor boy's body terribly mutilated. The Indians had beaten him over the head with their guns, and not satisfied with that, had stamped his insides out. The men got him onto a blanket and lifted him in on top of the hay. As luck would have it, they had turned the wagon around facing home before they picked the body up. They had no more got him in than the Indians attacked from the rear—came out of the brush, a dozen or more, shooting and whooping. The men put their horses in a fast run, shooting back all the time and trying to keep the poor dead boy from bouncing out of the wagon as they went over brush, gullies, and other obstructions that happened to be in the way. The Indians again followed them to within half a mile of the house. We could hear the shots, and excitement ran high. We youngsters were so terribly frightened that we tried every way to find a safe place to hide. Finally we decided that the safest place would be Cousin Jim's great old-fashioned fire place, which was nearly six feet wide. Running outside where Cousin Jim had two old cow hides stretched, we unstaked them, dragged them into the house, and put them up in front of the chimney. Then about seven of us crawled inside and tried to think we were safe.

The firing kept up. Father came into the house, called us all out, and made a speech to all the women and children, telling us that the first one that tried to run out of the house would be shot by him or some of the other men as they knew of the cruelty of the Indians and would a thousand times rather we would be killed than captured. We expected every moment that the Indians would make a rush on the ranch, but suddenly the shooting stopped and the men with the boy's body drove in. They felt sure they had killed some, but since Indians always carried their dead away, they couldn't be sure.

By this time it was getting dark and the people began bringing their horses in and tying them to the back yard fence, feeling sure of an attack before morning and not wishing to be left without horses to take them home when the time came to leave. And as Cousin Jim kept liquor as well as general merchandise in his store, most of the men began fortifying themselves for the fight they were expecting. Mother went out to them and asked them to please stop drinking lest they become too intoxicated to defend the women and children in the house. So they gave Mother the jug and before long were pretty sober.

They had placed a Mexican boy on top of the house to let them know when the Indians were coming, and about midnight they heard him cry, "They are coming! They are coming!"

Dad called out, "Everybody to arms, and find the safest place you can to shoot from!" Again he warned the women and children whatever happened not to leave the house.

By this time we could hear a clattering of horses' feet over the rocky hills. Everyone held his breath. Dad said, "Boys, hold your fire until they are close enough to see them." It was a beautiful moonlight night. Cousin Jim called to the boy on watch to hail them, so he did, in Spanish: "Who are you?" They answered in Spanish, "We are men." Then the boys asked if they shouldn't fire, but Cousin Jim called up, "Ask if they are friends." They answered, "We are."

It turned out they had heard the Indians were in, had gathered up their horses, and were bringing them in for safety. There were a dozen or more of them, and after they came we felt very safe as they were well armed.

Next day we wrapped the poor dead boy in sheeting from Cousin Jim's store, made a casket out of a piano box, and buried him. We felt sorry for his companion, who said it was going to be the hardest thing he ever did to go back and tell the parents of their son's terrible death.

The Indians seemed to come always when the moon shone. We lived in sight of the trail the Indians used when they came through our settlement, and I remember when Father was away how Mother would always don a pair of his trousers, take her Winchester, and parade around the yard to make the Indians (if any were in sight) think that men were there. They often came very near the house. One morning Father went out to bring the horses in and found two colts killed with arrows shot through them and still warm.

On one of their raids they surprised Kurg Ward, a neighbor of ours. About four of them made a charge, and as he bent low over his horse to avoid their arrows, one shot him between the shoulders, the arrow point showing through on the other side. The Indians ran him to within sight of the house, but he kept ahead of them. Dad and Dan Arnold pulled the arrow out, and though the wound was very painful, he soon recovered.

Bigfoot Wallace as a young man, Lexington, Virginia, 1869 (Western History Collections, University of Oklahoma).

OUR FRIEND BIGFOOT WALLACE

A<small>FTER THE KILLING</small> of the Webb boy the Indians committed other depredations and seemed to get worse all over the country. Our friend Bigfoot Wallace was living all alone on his ranch on the Chicon at the time and Father worried about him a great deal. After each raid he would go to see if Foot had been scalped yet. Finally, after one very ferocious attack, he got into his little green spring wagon one morning and set off to try to get the Captain to come and live with us, if he was still alive.

Captain Wallace needed protection from other things besides Indians at that time. A short time before he had been persuaded to let some rascal take all his fine herd of horses— several carloads—and ship them East to market; and neither the man nor the money ever came back. When Father heard of this he said he couldn't see any reason for Foot to live alone at the cabin any longer.

My sister Alice and I, who liked Mr. Wallace very much, were delighted to hear of the plan and for once hustled around helping Mother get ready for him. When his little room was fixed up and the afternoon was about over, we climbed on the high rail fence to watch and wait for him to come. It seemed we waited for hours before the little green wagon came around the bend, but finally we saw it driving up and there beside Father was the Captain in his long blue soldier overcoat, Kitty Sue, his favorite saddle horse, tied to the back of the wagon, and his two dogs, Sowder and Rock, following. My sister and I were not more than six or seven years old at the time.

From this time on Mr. Wallace took up his residence with our family. He would sometimes go over and stay with Uncle John and Aunt Sarah Thomas for a while and often visited them when he was staying with us. He always wanted Aunt Sarah to shave him and cut his hair.

We children always loved him dearly, and I think he was one of the kindest and most understanding men I ever knew. I can see since growing up how he studied each of the family and found out about their likes, dislikes, and dispositions. He always seemed to like me a great deal—I don't know why, unless he admired the way I always called a spade a spade and was always ready for a fight. It didn't take him long to find out that I was extremely fond of pets. The other children liked them too but didn't just live with them as I did, spending most of my time playing with and petting them. He never failed to bring me every young rabbit, squirrel, or anything else he came across—even to a javelina pig and a small black bear. That bear was the cutest thing. We had to keep it chained

John and Sarah Thomas, Aunt Fan's aunt and uncle, with their son, Walter, at the family home in Bigfoot, Texas. Bigfoot Wallace often stayed here. The photo was taken about 1881 (Courtesy of Sarah Thomas Maddox).

to a tree in the yard and it had a habit of walking just half way round the tree where it would turn a somersault, walk back to the starting point, turn another somersault, and start over, keeping that up for half a day at a time. Cubby wouldn't let anyone come near him but me and I loved him very dearly. Such shrieking and sobbing and carrying on as arose when he

Kinfolks. Walter Thomas, son of Uncle John and Aunt Sarah Thomas, was Aunt Fan's first cousin (Courtesy of Sarah Thomas Maddox).

died was never heard before. One night some lobo wolves came into the yard and killed him. My poor little Cubby! They had to promise me everything they could think of to still my shrieks. Not long after, Mr. Wallace tried to make it up to me by bringing me the javelina pig, but he was so mean I couldn't pet him, and anyway no pet I ever had could take the place of Cubby.

Sometimes Cap Wallace would let my sister Alice, my brother, and me go hunting with him for coons, wildcats, civet cats, and any of the other varmints with which the country abounded. I remember one day we were permitted to go with him when the dogs were baying. We found them around a tree barking at something. We all looked and could see nothing in the tree, so Mr. Wallace tried to call the dogs off. They would follow for a few yards, then go back to the tree again. I kept insisting there must be some cause for their persistence and on looking closely saw that part of the tree was hollow. Captain Wallace, feeling convinced that it was a false alarm, walked away, but I scaled up the trunk, and when the dogs saw me they came back again. I climbed up about twelve feet, thrust my hand into the hollow, and was nearly scared to death when a big raccoon jumped out right in my face. I was so badly frightened I turned all holds loose and tumbled down. I landed with the coon on top of me and the dogs on top of the coon. Cap Wallace had to come and rescue me and was as mad as a hornet. He told me I'd get into bad trouble some day because of my hard-headedness. I've thought of what he said many times since and know that I would have come out better oftentimes if I had been more tractable. On this occasion I do think Cap was just a little annoyed because I was right about that tree after he had ordered us to abandon it.

We children used to love to sit on our old gallery and listen to the stories Mr. Wallace would tell us. He had many tales about the days when he drove the stage from San Antonio to El Paso and was often attacked by the Indians. Sometimes he would tell us about his hunting expeditions. One story I don't remember seeing in print is about his great friend

Dutch Pete. It happened while he was living on his Chicon ranch. It seems that Cap Wallace, Pete, and a couple more whose names I've forgotten started out on a hunt, and after hunting all day found a little cabin out in the woods where they decided they would spend the night. The cabin had several wide planks laid up across the rafters, not extending all the way across but leaving some loose ends about six feet long which didn't quite reach the last rafter. To get out of the way of skunks, snakes, and such, they climbed up on those planks and spread their blankets. They had turned in and were almost asleep when six big Indians came into the cabin, built a fire in the chimney, and proceeded to broil a deer they had killed. Of course all those who were asleep awoke at once. Pete was so full of curiosity he just couldn't be still and kept crawling over and peeping to see what the Indians were doing. The others would catch him by the seat of his pants and pull him back, but he'd creep over again, edging all the time toward where the planks were loose. Finally he got too near; the planks kicked up; and Pete landed right in the midst of the Indians. The rest, feeling "the jig was up," let out war whoops, jumped down, and began firing their rifles. Every Indian took to his heels and to the brush, leaving guns, bows and arrows, and (best of all) the deer meat broiled to a turn. "By Gor," Bigfoot would exclaim, "that was the best meat I ever tasted!"

It was this same Dutch Pete who accompanied Bigfoot one time on a trip with the El Paso stage. He was sleeping on the ground under the stage one night when the Indians attacked. Pete was very much excited. In his eagerness to get a shot at the attackers he thrust his head between the spokes of a wheel and nearly overturned the coach trying to get it out. He was armed only with a derringer but he tried to put it to use and pulled the trigger three times without getting any results. Disgusted, he put the derringer back into his pocket and immediately it fired all by itself, grazing his leg and throwing him into something like a fit. "Got for damn!" he yelled. "I make you off three times and you no go off. I put you in my pocket and you make off!"

Ed Westfall, Bigfoot Wallace's companion in many a frontier adventure (The University of Texas at Austin, Eugene C. Barker Texas History Center).

Another of the Captain's stories was about the time he and his friend Westfall were in El Paso, having landed there in the stage coach. They happened to go down to the bank of the Rio Grande where at that time there was not much chance of crossing except when Mexican men hired out to carry the women across on their backs, and Bigfoot, having a great sense of humor, thought it would be good sport to participate. The women were paying two "clackos" (pieces of money about the equivalent of a penny) to get someone to take them across, so Bigfoot says, "Westfall, here's where we come in." They picked them a good fat one apiece, got them on their backs, took them to where the water was deepest, and then started pitching like a couple of horses. Mr. Wallace said he never pitched so hard and reared so high in all his life before he finally dislodged the fair damsel right out in the middle of the stream. He said he was sorry of his bargain before he finished his job, as he lost at least a dollar's worth of hair— said she came near leaving him bald-headed.

He would tell us about the time he and Westfall were in a tight place in an Indian fight, and as they jumped over a brush fence he ran his ramrod into Westfall's eye. Westfall remarked, "This is a hell of a place to punch a fellow's eye out!"

Then there was his little Indian girl, Chapita, who clung to his shirt tail all during a battle with her people, crying "Capitan Wallicky, Capitan Wallicky!" He used to say, "By Gor, I hated to leave that little girl there, for I knew she would be punished when her people, who had taken to the woods, got back again."

We would sit and listen to his tales with eyes and mouths wide open and would sit up all night if he would keep on telling them—and then be afraid to go to bed. He would say, "Now go to bed! There are no Indians here now, and if you don't stop acting so silly I'm not going to tell you any more stories." Then we would assure him that we weren't the least bit afraid—we just weren't sleepy. And so next night we would get him by the hand and pull him out on the porch to tell us some more stories.

In spite of his many wild adventures he was of a very

mild disposition and loved to be helpful around the house and garden. He loved to plant and see things grow and was a wonder at "hog-killing time," assisting with the killing and afterward with the cutting, smoking, sausage making, lard rendering, and so on. And he was really something when it came to killing game and bringing it in already skinned or picked and ready to be cooked. Mother was sometimes annoyed at him—for instance when he came to the table with Rock on one side and Sowder on the other. As he ate he would give first one and then the other a bite of the choicest meat, cake, bread, or anything he thought they would like best. Mother never uttered one word of protest and he had no idea she disliked his bringing his dogs in and feeding them at the table. Our dogs always stayed outside and were never allowed in the house.

Occasionally he left us to go to conventions, meetings of old soldiers, and such. He never came home from one of these trips without bringing a load of fruit and candy tied up in his large bandanna handkerchief. I remember especially well one time when he attended the Battle of Flowers in San Antonio, a celebration which is always held on the anniversary of the Battle of San Jacinto. He left home in his ordinary "Sunday clothes," as he called the ones he reserved for best wear (still, they weren't so hot). I recall vividly his return about a week later. A carriage drove up in front of the house and a gentleman stepped out with a long-tailed, fine black broadcloth coat on (the kind the old Southern colonels used to wear) and pants and vest to match. He was wearing a black tie and black shoes shined so bright they hurt your eyes, carried a beautiful gold-headed cane, and, to top it all, had on one of those high silk hats. We all started bustling around, grabbing something decent to put on, feeling sure it was some of Dad's aristocratic kindred from Virginia coming to visit him. We had just had a shock from one of them a short time before. After getting somewhat prettied up, we peeked out the door and lo and behold! it was Captain Wallace returning from the Battle of the Flowers. His old cronies in San Antonio had had a special float made, all flower-bedecked and with a large decorated

Bigfoot Wallace dressed up for a convention (The University of Texas at Austin, Eugene C. Barker Texas History Center).

throne on it, and had arranged to have old Bigfoot perch up there in the midst, the only thing on the float. A large sign over his head was inscribed: OUR TEXAS HERO—BIG-FOOT WALLACE. He reported having a wonderful time but called for his favorite chair and said, "Let me set down and cool my feet." The fine shoes came off, and it didn't take him long to get out of his finery and into his daily attire.

Bigfoot was not a drinking man, but when celebrating with his old comrades he would come home slightly inebriated. He always said he was "completely depleted," but I always called it something else. It didn't take long for him to perk up and start work in the garden, which he loved to do, and I'll wager he bought a car load of garden seeds in his lifetime.

I remember so many little incidents that happened while he was with us. There was one in particular that always tickled me. He always subscribed to the San Antonio *Express* and the Houston *Post*, and we girls found a special use for his papers. I had grown up until I thought I was a young lady, and in those days ladies wore bustles. The bigger the bustle the more stylish the lady. I tried to make mine as large as decency would permit, and found I could make a very nice-sized one with a newspaper tied on a string and all puffed out. Captain Wallace got onto it some way and when he missed his paper would always ask, "Fan, what's the date of your latest bustle?"

I remember with amusement also how he kept a cedar water bucket hanging out in the arbor back of the kitchen to keep his drinking water cool. Nearby was a water gourd he used as a cup. One day a Mexican we had working in the fields whom the Captain disliked (he disliked all Mexicans because his memories were still vivid) came in from the field and, seeing no one near, rammed his head into the bucket to get a drink. Just as he got his head under the bail of the bucket, Captain Wallace happened by. Uttering oaths with vehemence, the Captain gave him such a kick in the pants that the Mexican reared back. As he did so the bail jerked off the hook and fell over his neck. There they ran across the fields, the Mexican with the bucket around his neck splashing water, the Captain right behind kicking him at every step. The Mexican finally dislodged the bucket and ran off across the prairie, which was the last we ever saw of him. Mr. Wallace came back carrying the bucket and said, "God damn! I've not killed half enough Mexicans yet!"

For two generations he took as much interest in wielding the rod as the parents did in our family. He had a habit of going down to the tank we had for watering the cattle to take his bath. He would take an old leather-bottomed chair, wade out until the water was about waist deep, and then sit in the chair and bathe. When my son Ewell Cochran and my nephew Gus Leuthy were about nine years old, they thought it would be great fun to hide in the surrounding brush and shoot as near to him as they could with their "nigger shooters." They thought this would make him believe the Indians were after him. The old Captain never said a word or let on that anything was happening, but calmly finished his bath, dressed, and came back to the house. On the way, however, he got a nice, long, flat board which he hid in his shirt. Tilting his chair back against the kitchen door, he opened up his newspaper and began to read, all the while keeping one of his eagle eyes out for "the scamps," as he called them.

After sneaking around for a while, the boys saw the Captain reading the paper and thought he had forgotten all about the Indian playing. Anyway, it was about time for lunch, so the young men ventured in. The Captain sat perfectly still until they were about even with him; then he reached out those long arms and grabbed both of them. He put one small boy's head between his legs, holding him like a vise while he "poured it on" the other one. Then he turned him loose and served the other likewise.

The young men felt very much "sat upon" so they started looking for some way to get even. Now the Captain was very much interested in raising fine chickens, and whenever he found anyone having extra good ones, he would get a setting of eggs, bring them home, and set them under one of his own setting hens. In this way he had built up a flock of fine chickens. He doted on one especially noble rooster and had often taken the boys out to ask them if they had ever seen anything so beautiful anywhere else in the country. Still smarting from the indignity of the Indian escapade, they decided that an injury to the rooster would really aggravate the old man; so they caught Mr. Rooster and pulled off every feather, leaving only the long tail feathers.

It wasn't long before Mr. Wallace spied his rooster and called the whole family out to see the wreck. When I saw what had happened I said, "Captain, I'll beat the dickens out of those youngsters," and he replied, "Don't. I want to attend to them myself. What I want you to do is get something to make him a coat so the sun won't burn him." We made him the coat, and with the Captain herding him under the shade, it wasn't long until he was again covered with beautiful feathers, and the new ones were so much prettier than the old that the Captain said, "By Gor, I think I'll pick the whole flock!" Needless to say, he attended adequately to the boys, who about gave up trying to get ahead of the old man.

He always made much ado about his birthday. I believe if he had been on the Sahara Desert he would have found some means of celebrating. That was one time he would always have his jug of whiskey. He said he was born at fifteen minutes past five in the morning and that the midwife said he could kick harder and yell louder than any young one she ever saw. I could always depend on his call at four-thirty: "Fan, Fan, get up! The baby is going to want his tea" (as he called the birthday refreshments). Then I would get up and make the eggnog he always insisted on having, and meanwhile he would arouse the rest of the family; but not one drink would he allow to be served until exactly fifteen minutes after five o'clock. Then he would cut the birthday cake and drink to the health of "the baby."

When I finally had a home of my own, the Captain came to spend his last years with me. He had some land certificates which could be laid on land anywhere in Texas, so he engaged a lawyer in Galveston who told him he could make him a wealthy man. All he had to do was to turn everything over to this lawyer (whose name was Maddox) and give him power of attorney. Maddox laid a part of the certificates over some part of Galveston which he claimed still belonged to Texas, though the government had built wharves and other expensive buildings on it, and part on some land at Aransas Pass. After a while Mr. Wallace got disgusted because he felt he had been "done" again by another shark, so he said, "Fan, I'll never live to get anything out of this deal, and if you want it, I'll deed the whole thing to you, though I don't think it will ever amount to anything." Father was in my house at the time and said, "Well, I'll draw up a deed if you want it that way, Foot." So he did. Just a short time afterward a friend of mine, Colonel George Holcombe, came with Mrs. Holcombe to spend a week or two as people did in those days and I told him about the deed. Captain Wallace, Dad, Colonel Holcombe, and I talked it over and decided that Colonel Holcombe should go to Aransas Pass and see what could be done. While there he sold the land and brought the money back. After a conference with Mr. Wallace, we decided to build a new house on my farm, and the Captain, who had been living with me for years, spent his last days there.

Colonel Holcombe was the publisher of the Devine *News* and also published the life of Bigfoot Wallace written by A. J. Sowell. When he sold the *News* and was getting ready to go to Luling to take charge of the paper there, he came to spend a while with me and brought Sowell's book, just off the press. They folded and got the book ready for binding while they were with me, and Mr. Wallace died while they were there.

My husband, W. W. Cochran, was away just then and it was mighty nice to have someone there at the time of Mr. Wallace's illness and death. He had been feeling bad for several days but was never confined to his bed—ran a slight temperature and seemed to have some cold, but never appeared alarmingly ill. The day before he died he said he was feeling much better and sat out in the yard in his chair, which he liked to lean up against the wall. When he came in, he and Father and Colonel Holcombe sat up late talking in the front room where I had put a single bed for Mr. Wallace because of the fire in the fireplace there. He seemed to sleep well that night. I

J. J. (Jack) Sowell, Bigfoot Wallace's biographer (Western History Collections, University of Oklahoma).

was in the habit of going in through the night to see if he wanted water or anything since he had been having the cold. The morning he died my father had come, as he usually did, to get his cup of coffee early, and he and Colonel Holcombe and Mr. Wallace were talking, Mr. Wallace still sitting on his bed and putting on his shoes. I had gone into the kitchen when I heard Daddy say, "Foot, Foot! What's the matter?" I ran in to see, and Dad and Colonel Holcombe were laying him back on the bed. Colonel Holcombe said, "He's gone."

I tried to argue that he couldn't be dead so quickly, but he was, poor old dear, and the next day we took him and buried him in the graveyard at Longview Cemetery. In about a month his body was taken up and taken to Austin where he was buried with military honors.

I have learned many things about him since his death. Just lately I heard that he dug the first well ever put down in Austin, Texas. He asked a saloon man there why he hauled his drinking water from the Colorado River. The man told him it was because they could get no other water there. Bigfoot told him if he would furnish two men as helpers he would insure him water at a dollar a foot—no water, no pay; and he would pay the help if he didn't get water. Mr. Wallace got good water at fifty feet. He also killed the last two buffalo that were ever seen in the vicinity of Austin.

People in those days were very different from what they are now. There was never any question of remuneration for anything. All the years that Bigfoot lived with us there was never any thought of his paying board. And he was not the only one. Others would come and stay for a month or two, and even longer, and I really think it would have been taken as an insult if they had offered payment for being taken care of. I am still shocked when I hear people complain that their house-guests stay too long. I wish we could have kept the old Captain longer than we did.

HIGH WATER

THE CAPTAIN went through a great many ups and downs with our family. One of the worst was a drouth which occurred not long after he came to our house to live. It hadn't rained for several months; the grass had all dried up; the water holes were all dry. They had been watering stock at the wells for some time but it was a slow go for so many cattle so the men folks went down to the San Miguel, where there was still some grass, prickly pear, and water, and built a shack with a place to cook and eat outside under the trees. The cattle were rounded up and driven over and then we all got aboard the spring wagon to go to our temporary home. We found two covered wagons drawn up beside the shack and everything in readiness for the family.

Dad hired a bunch of Mexicans to burn prickly pear for the cattle, and with what grass there was and plenty of water, the cattle seemed to get along fine.

But the family wasn't destined to fare so well. We hadn't been there very long when one day my little sister Jennie, who was playing in the shack, stooped down by a trunk sitting at the back and an enormous rattlesnake about six feet long struck at her. The fangs fastened in her panties right in front. The cloth was loose, since she was bending over, and as fortune would have it her flesh was not penetrated. She ran out screaming, dragging the snake. Mr. Wallace saw her predicament and with his usual presence of mind jumped in the middle of the snake and tore him loose; then, quickly putting a big foot on the snake's head, soon exterminated him.

Soon after the snake episode Mr. Wallace permitted us

children to go out with him where the dogs had treed a wild cat, he taking his gun to shoot the creature out of the tree. Just as we got under the tree on the other side from the dogs, the old cat made a leap from the branches, ran right between little sister Jennie's legs and carried her off on his back, to the amusement of the rest of us children. Mr. Wallace took after the cat and Jennie, but before he overhauled them the beast dislodged her, leaving her perfectly safe and sound but frightened half to death. We youngsters thought it was awfully funny but got a good scolding from the Captain who, I think, was frightened himself. He never afterwards would let us accompany him on his hunting sprees.

This did not prevent little sister Jennie from deciding one morning that she would go on a hunting trip of her own. Unknown to the family, she took the two dogs Nick and Bravo and started out. She had not proceeded very far when the dogs ran onto a bunch of javelinas which went after her. Small as she was, she knew how to scale up into a nearby mesquite tree, but the limb she climbed out on was partly rotted away and broke off. As luck would have it, the tail of her dress caught over the stump of the limb as she started falling and there she swung. Her yells attracted Mr. Wallace, who was out hunting his horse. He hastily grabbed up a mesquite club and came to her rescue. Taking her down from the broken limb, he told her to hang onto his back while he beat off the ferocious little creatures with the club and his big brogans. Finally he got her safely back to camp where he gave her a couple of spats on the behind and told her if he ever caught her out with the dogs again, she would get a lot more of the same.

We hadn't been living in our shack on the San Miguel a great while when one night it started raining, and I don't think I ever witnessed such a downpour. It rained all night and all the next day. We were located in a low place and the downpour continued until we could hardly see more than a few yards from the shack. Quite late in the evening one of the men ventured out and hurried back to tell us we were almost surrounded by water and had better try to get to higher ground.

We decided to make for a little knoll some distance from where we were and began gathering up some things to take along. There were a frying pan, a coffee pot, and, luckily for us, a large stew pan in which we carried some of our groceries. The men rolled up our bedding in canvas and, making as many trips as they could before the water got too high, managed to carry it to the high ground along with enough corn meal, lard, coffee, and bacon to keep us from getting too hungry.

We all got safely to the knoll and then the men began dragging up wood to our camping place so as to have a fire if the rain ever stopped and a fire could be made to burn.

The water kept coming nearer and nearer. It seemed that it was coming down from some of the creeks that led into the San Miguel as well as pouring down from the sky. When at last it stopped rising there was a place about fifty yards square left above the water level, and all around in every direction water was all you could see.

There were two fair-sized trees on our camping place, and Father and Captain Wallace got the ropes off the bed rolls to tie us children to the branches, for they knew we were going to have to spend the night there and if the water kept on rising we would all have to take to the trees. Fortunately for us the rain stopped early in the night and the water began to recede. After many trials they got the fire going, which certainly was welcome as everybody was wet to the skin.

All during the time the water was rising rabbits, rattlesnakes, and rats kept trying to join us on our little camping place—the only spot in the neighborhood not covered with water. The men folks kept guard with clubs, killing snakes and rats. I think they must have killed fifty rattlesnakes and numerous rats. The rabbits came in handy, for all our eatables were soon consumed except the cornmeal. Mother would fill the large stew pan with water, stir in the cornmeal, and cook the rabbits in the mixture. Fortunately we still had salt, and we were so hungry we consumed the concoction with great gusto. As I think of it now, it seems anything but appetizing.

We were stranded on that little island three days and

nights before the water went down enough so we could get out.

When the flood first began Father and Mr. Wallace had gone back to turn the cows and calves out of the pen so they could swim to safety. The water was up to their arm pits when they reached the shack, and Mr. Wallace insisted on tying the covered wagon in which he slept to a tree so it wouldn't be washed away. However, he tied only the wheels and axles to the trees, and imagine his dismay when he found, after the water receded, that the wheels were still there but the bed had been washed away with his clothing, bedding, and all his little belongings. And do you know, although they searched far and wide for the wagon bed, they could never find a trace of it until several months later when some cow hunters came and told Cap Wallace they had found his wagon away up in the top of a tree. It had hung on the stump of a tree which someone had cut the top off of, probably looking for a bee's nest. Of course all his effects had washed out and gone.

On the evening our trouble began two of my cousins, Marion and Wallis Thomas, had come to spend the night with us and of course were with us through it all. They had ridden double on a little roan cow pony and had staked him out not a great way from the place where we took refuge. In the excitement everyone forgot the poor pony, and when we did think of him we could just see his head and shoulders above the water. Of course we children couldn't stand that, and the four of us started out to the rescue. Although the eldest wasn't more than thirteen years old, we were all good swimmers, so we stripped down to our underwear and started what was really a hazardous undertaking. Our departure was unbeknown to the family, who were all busy trying to fix a place to cook and eat as it was getting late in the day and everybody was hungry, especially Mr. Wallace.

By this time in the deeper parts of the creek bottom the trees were covered to their tops, and great logs were washing down the current. If one had struck us we never would have known what happened, but we kept on going, taking hold of branches of trees as we went. Sometimes we would go clear under the water, but on we went.

Just before we reached the pony, the grown-ups missed us, looked around and saw us clinging to the trees, and started shrieking for us to stay where we were. Cap Wallace, being the tallest man there, started out after us. He managed to untie the horse and then, taking us one at a time, finally got us to the camp. I still believe if they had let us alone we would have got out, for none of us was the least bit excited and we all were good swimmers and accustomed to the water.

The horse, when released, made tracks for my uncle's place. He had to swim a very long way, but finally got to Uncle John's house and caused a great deal of worry. On finding out that the San Miguel was on the rampage, it didn't take Uncle John long to saddle up and make his way as near as he could to where we were. He couldn't come very close, for we were entirely surrounded by water, so he went home and reported that he thought we had all been washed away. In order to make sure, he got several of the neighbors to help him and they made another attempt at reaching us, this time coming close enough so that some of the men thought they could hear someone calling. They all listened, and heard a faint, far-away voice. Then they sent up regular Indian war whoops and finally got an answer. It was impossible for them to identify the voice, but Uncle John had heard enough to convince him that some of us at least were alive, and so they came back next day to try again.

By then the water had receded enough so we could get near enough to talk to them. In fact we had already waded back to the wreck where our shack had been. Not a vestige of clothing or anything was left; one of the cows and two calves were never heard of again; and another cow was later found twenty miles below where we camped.

Uncle John had brought a stake rope with him, and finding a narrow place in the creek where a dead tree had washed up so as to make a bridge part way across, he had Father come out as far as he could on the tree and catch the end of the rope.

Then we all went out one at a time to Father, who tied the rope around us. When each was ready, Uncle would say "Jump," and they would pull us across. We children thought it was great sport, and it never entered our heads that even that process was dangerous, with the water still raging down the creek.

We all got across wet as drowned rats and hungry as bears and were grateful for a ride in Uncle's farm wagon, which he had brought to take us back in. Aunt Sarah had a nice warm meal and some dry clothes for us.

So ended our stay on the San Miguel, but the men had to go back and look after the cattle until the grass put up on the home ranch, which didn't take long for the spring rains had begun in earnest.

FRONTIER CHILDHOOD

Pᴇᴏᴘʟᴇ ɪɴ ᴛʜᴏsᴇ ᴅᴀʏs believed in "bringing children up in the way they should go," and never "spared the rod." Visitors always got a great kick out of the way Father chastised us youngsters. He would start in on Monday laying up our misdemeanors against us, telling us, "You'll be punished for this next Sunday morning." And he never forgot. After breakfast every Sunday morning he would herd us out to a great big oak tree in the yard, cut some nice, keen switches, and start operations. I remember I always begged to be first, and the wish was usually granted as the others wanted their punishment delayed as long as possible.

People these days talk about how mean the children have got to be—if there are any nearly as bad as we were, they are in some house of correction. It couldn't be laid at the door of our parents, for we were as meek as lambs as long as we were around them and were very careful never to let them know about the things we did, for we knew what was coming when and if they found out.

I got Sunday morning dressings for fighting more than for anything else. When I'd see a youngster, the first thing I'd do would be to size him up, and if he wasn't too big I'd walk up and give him a dig in the nose. Then the battle would come off. Sometimes I'd get licked, and other times I'd come off victorious. I can't imagine to this day why I wanted to do it. I remember once Father called me up and said, "Fan, a lady and a man are coming over to spend the day. They are good friends of mine. They have two little boys and I want you to be nice to them and not fight them." (Dad knew how mean I

Texas tomboy—Fan Bramlette ready for battle (Frances Bramlette Far-ris Collection).

was about fighting.) I never said yea or nay but just waited until the visitors arrived. I watched them get out of their hack and sized the boys up. One was somewhat larger than I and the other smaller, but I had gained a lot of confidence in my fighting powers and was sure I could best the two of them if I had to. After some maneuvering I got them out to play, and Dad, knowing me, said, "Now Fan, play nice!" But Fan had other ideas. Persuading them out behind the cow pen, I tackled the biggest one with my fist. I gave him one on the nose, and gosh, he went after me like a whirlwind—knocked me down and then got hold of a mesquite brush, thorns and all. When he quit, I was a very subdued young lady, all skinned up and my nose bleeding. Of course the young men told all about it and Father never forgot to tease me about it to his dying day.

I remember one boy I was afraid to tackle. His name was Simps McCoy and he was one of the wildest kids I ever saw. He came to our place with his grandfather, and before he lit off his horse he was challenging anyone who wanted to fight. Then he took his lariat off his saddle and made a run at my sister and me, trying to rope us. After a hard chase he succeeded in catching my sister, and started in yelling, "Roped a gal, Daddy, roped a gal, Daddy!" That was one time little Fannie didn't interfere or take her sister's part.

My father was very bald-headed—had only a fringe of hair around his head. He liked to take an afternoon siesta and was lying out on a cot under trees when young McCoy spied him. He walked up, stood and viewed him a few minutes, and finally said, "Scalded and scraped, by God." In those days they killed many hogs for meat and would scrape the hair off after scalding them in a barrel of boiling water. I don't suppose Simps had ever seen a bald-headed man before.

By this time my little brother had grown into quite a boy, though he was still young enough for us to teach him meanness. We were into anything that youngsters could think of. We would ride any kind of animal that wore hair. I remember the men had made a gate to the cow lot and had put an arch over it. We would take turns about climbing up on the arch while the other two drove the steers through the gate. The one overhead would swing off onto a steer's back and ride as far as possible before being pitched off. Then we would drive the steers back and another would take his turn. I've often wondered how we ever lasted to grow up.

At this time, when I was about five or six years old, my sister and I would go out into the pasture where we had some very wild cattle. If we could manage it before starting out, we would put on red dresses; and if we couldn't do that, we would get any red cloth—bandanna handkerchiefs or whatever we could find. Then we would go forth to the pasture, climb through the fence, and start bawling like a calf to attract the cows. We would stand twenty-five or thirty yards inside the pasture and dare the cattle until they would take after us, just pawing the dirt and snorting. Then we'd run back and climb over the fence before they could catch us. We thought that was great sport and kept it up for several days, but one day I must have gone farther from the fence than I thought or else the cow ran faster than usual. Anyway she hitched her horn in my belt. In those days we wore strong gingham dresses with belts fastened firmly around the waist. She carried me I suppose about fifty yards, slinging up her head, snorting and bawling. When she finally dislodged me she lost no time in following the bunch, and I went home a wiser child where cows were concerned.

It was not long after this episode that I had my first experience with a train. The International and Great Northern Railroad was being built from Laredo to San Antonio and would pass at its nearest point about seven miles from where we were living. We had never seen a train and Father asked us if we would like to go and watch one pass through. Of course we were very anxious to make the trip, so he got the bunch together. A family named Laxson had moved into the neighborhood, including two girls about the age of my sister and myself. We took them and a grown sister who was blind and drove over to the tracks. We found them running through a cut between embankments about fourteen feet high, and there we all perched to wait for the train, Father urging us all the time not to get too close. We thought the train would never come. It grew dark, and still we waited. Finally Father said, "I can hear the roar. The train will be here in a few minutes." We stood up, all excited, and pretty soon here she came, clanging and puffing, her big red eye shining.

We stood it until she was within about a hundred feet of us, and then every fellow took to his heels. We scattered in all directions, leaving the poor blind girl to her fate. She tried to run too, fell over the embankment, and rolled clear to the bottom. They had quite a time rounding us all up, and we had seen all the trains we cared to for some time to come.

It was wonderful to have the Laxson girls for neighbors. We were so happy to have someone near our age to play with, and we soon began having a lot of fun and adventures together. We ran away from our long-suffering parents, climbed trees, and went swimming in the water holes which abounded there and were sometimes deep enough to be dangerous. Our mothers called us in one day and laid down the law to us— told us what they would do to us if we came in once more with our clothes torn from climbing trees.

There was a large oak tree about a mile from where we lived, completely covered with a mustang grape vine. We had been planning for some time to go to that grape vine and get some grapes, but after our lecture we were afraid to venture forth for fear we might go back home with our clothes torn. What were we to do? We just couldn't give up going, and there would be no use going unless we could get some grapes. And we couldn't get the grapes without climbing the tree. I, though the youngest, was always the first to propose any devilment, and finally I said, "I know what. We can go to the tree and get up among the thick grape vines and take our clothes off. The vines are so thick no one could see us anyway."

All consented, and up we went like so many squirrels. When we got up a little way, we pulled off every rag and threw them down under the tree. Then up we went to the very top and were having such a good time eating grapes and visiting that we had no idea how long we were staying. At last our parents got worried about us and sent one of the girls' brothers, about eighteen years old, out to see if the Indians had got us. I think we must have given a hint to the family that some day we were going to that grape vine. Anyway the boy looked for us there, and when we heard a horseman ride up under the tree we were just frightened stiff, thinking it was Indians. When we found out who it was we almost wished it had been Indians.

He yelled, "Oh, yes, I've found you!" We hid under the foliage, but he knew we were there, and *undressed*, for our clothes were under the tree. And do you know, that rascal gathered our clothes up and took them home, leaving us there just as we were born.

It seemed as if we were destined to spend the night up there *sin ropa*, but just before dark Father and Mr. Wallace rode up with our raiment. Father told us to come down, get into our clothes, and beat it home, and it didn't take us long to comply. Dad and Captain Wallace rode on and waited for us, and I was sure of another Sunday morning dressing, but Cap interceded for us and we got off. Cap Wallace said, "Fan, I'll bet you were instigator of this." I always got the credit for all the meanness, whether guilty or innocent.

Cap Wallace loved to grow gourds and grew many kinds, among them those immense bottle gourds which would hold at least a gallon of water. They were funny looking, like two big round gourds connected in the center by a small neck. The Mexicans often used them to carry water when they rode on horseback, filling them with water and hanging them to the horn of the saddle by a leather thong tied to the neck in the middle. Cap Wallace had a lot of them around the house. We children would slip them out and take them to the branch (water hole) with us. We would put them under our arms and they buoyed us up and helped a lot in swimming. One day while Mother was away from the house my sister Alice, brother Pat, and I gathered a couple of gourds each and started out to our favorite swimming pool. After we had been swimming for a while with the gourds tied under our arms, Sister Alice said, "I bet I can walk on the water like Christ did." Brother and I were too busy with our own fun to pay much attention to her. First thing we knew we heard a splash, and looking around saw two big gourds floating and splashing around in the water with two feet tied to them flaying and bouncing. Alice's head was somewhere down below. Crazy-like, we thought that was about the funniest sight we ever saw and nearly split our sides laughing until finally we decided we had better do something. The water was deep, and before we could get her out she came near drowning all three of us. She was perfectly helpless, and the pull of the gourds was so strong, it was quite a task to get her right side up, but after a long time we succeeded. She was so exhausted we thought we would never get her home.

We didn't dare let Mother know of our escapade and never breathed a word until some time later when Mr. Wallace

started hunting for his gourds and asked us if we knew anything about them. As mean a set of brats as we were, we
wouldn't lie about anything, so we got the Captain away
from where Mother was and told him about our adventure.
When he found we had left his gourds on the bank, he told
Mother he would take us for a walk. We went back to the
place and the gourds were still there, right where we had
left them. Cap Wallace never gave us away. We could always
tell him anything and he would help us out of our childish
troubles without betraying our secrets.

Shortly after our gourd experience one of our friends was
drowned in that same water hole. Johnny McMahon and
George Holmes went in swimming there. Johnny dived in,
struck his head against a rock, and never came to the surface.
They found him wedged between two rocks. He was a
brother to Uncle Sam Thomas's wife, Aunt Mary.

Uncle Sam's marriage, I remember, was another thing
that brought out the worst in me. We dearly loved Uncle
Sam, who had been with us since we were born and had loved
and coddled us all our lives. For a few years we tagged after
him wherever he went and we had him all to ourselves; but
there came a time when a charming young lady moved with
her family into our settlement and Uncle seemed to like her
company very much. She came to visit with Mother often
and since she always noticed my sister and me, we began to
think she was quite all right. Then one day we heard Mother
ask Uncle Sam if they were planning on being married right
away—and the crying and bawling began to come off. We
yelled and shrieked until Mother had to take a hand to quell
us. We yelped and begged Uncle Sam not to leave us, and for
several days we moped around, red-eyed, hardly speaking to
him. When the young lady came to visit Mother, we would
get behind the large oak tree and shake our fists and make
faces at her, always being careful that Mother or Uncle didn't
see us. I remember one time she came, and I went away down
the road to waylay her as she went home. I was going to tell
her what I thought about her trying to marry our Uncle Sam.
I sat there in the sun for what seemed an awfully long time.

Finally she came, but imagine my consternation when I saw that Uncle Sam was with her. He asked what on earth I was doing away out there alone—didn't I know the Indians might get me? I started squalling, saying I wanted the Indians to get me. He wanted to know why. I said, "You know why! Because that hateful Mary is going to take you away and we will never see you any more, and I wanted to stay here and ask her to please not marry you." I was in such a state of hysterics that they took me back to the house and were kinder to me than I deserved.

Then Sister and I began wondering and planning what we could do to prevent the marriage. Uncle Sam had gone to San Antonio and bought a very pretty suit for his wedding. He had it locked up in his trunk and kept the key in his trousers pocket. We stayed awake one night, crept in to where he slept, and slipped the key out of his pocket. Next morning as soon as the family was outside we unlocked his trunk and poured a pan full of dirt over the suit and all his wedding clothes, thinking now he surely couldn't marry. And like the little demons we were we went out to where he was in the field and told him we came to bring him his key we had found on the floor of his room where he slept. He was sweet to us and said we were so nice to bring him his key. He even picked us up and let us ride his oxen with which he was plowing. We stayed out in the field with him a long time—until he decided to go to the house and get a drink of water. While there he went to his room, saw some sand on top of his trunk, and became suspicious. So he unlocked the trunk and, awful to behold, there was his wedding suit all covered with sand and dirt, his white shirt a mess, and his tie twisted into a knot. He raised up from the trunk and never said a word—just took us both by the hand and led us out to the same oak tree that Father took us to for our Sunday morning dressings. There, as the cowboys say, he "laid it into us." After that we decided there was nothing we could do but let the wedding go on.

When they were married Uncle Sam filed on a homestead and lived quite near us. As soon as we got over our tantrums we began to like our new aunt very much, and after we had grown up we never had a better friend than Aunt Mary. Long years afterward I asked her what she thought of the way my sister and I treated her when we were small. She said she didn't blame us. If anyone tried to take him from her she would resent it just as much or more.

While all this was going on our parents were thinking something should be done about our education. There was no possible chance for a school near us as yet, and though Father wanted to send us to San Antonio to the convent, Mother wouldn't hear of the idea. She wanted to keep us as near her as possible and would never consent to being separated from us. So Father began looking about for someone to tutor us and finally found a man in San Antonio by the name of Jim Dawson who was willing to risk the Indians, desperadoes, and wild animals. So began our education. Mr. Dawson stayed with us for almost a year. Then the same thing had to be gone over again, and we had Judge Lackey. When he had enough of the Wild West, we got a little bald-headed man named Leonidas Smith. We liked Mr. Smith very much. He played with us and often when the moon was shining bright, as it can shine only in that beautiful old country, Mr. Smith would take us out in the yard and sing something that began with "There's a rose in the garden for you, young man," and something about "You promised to marry me a year or so ago. I hold you to your promise and you can't say no." I've often tried to think of the balance of that play. I know we would hop and jump around singing and thought we were having a wonderful time. Bigfoot Wallace would come to visit us (it was before he came to live with us) and would laugh at our capers.

After Mr. Smith left us we had our first regular school-ing. We had built a small, one-room schoolhouse and hired a teacher, Miss Fannie McMahon, to teach a three-months term. We liked Miss Fannie very much. She was a niece of Judge John McMahon and of Mrs. James Speed. The McMahons and Speeds were newcomers to the settlement. I shall always remember Grandmother Speed, Mr. James Speed's mother, what an elegant old lady she was and how she always dressed in a beautiful black taffeta dress with such dainty little black or white lace caps. Elderly ladies wore them in those days but they were rare in frontier homes—so much so that we regarded Mother Speed as very much out of the ordinary. She was one of the finest women I ever knew. I don't think she ever said an unkind word of anyone, and she would tell us children, "If you can't say anything good of people, just don't say anything." And I think if that attitude were taken all over the world, it would be a better place to live in.

The schoolhouse the settlers built was near the Laxson home, and we children had to pass by their place to get to school. For some unknown reason we almost always had our two dogs follow us to school, and one morning after the two Laxson girls had spent the night with us we started out as usual with the two dogs following. On this day we had taken our baby sister, about five years old, along with us. Just before we got to the Laxson house we had to pass through a heavily overgrown chaparral thicket, and as we came along the dogs bayed a bunch of javelina hogs. When the javelinas made a rush the dogs ran to where we were, the hogs following and snapping at them every jump. We saw our danger and started running as fast as we could, trying to get to a corn pen the Laxsons had built just outside their field fence and about a hundred yards from their house. By the time we reached it there must have been at least fifty of those vicious little beasts right at our heels. They had all gathered when they heard the fight between their companions and the dogs.

We just did get to the pen and up out of their reach by the time they caught up with us. There they were just beneath our heels and making the most awful noise—*sweetch, sweetch*—which seemed to come from their bristles. Their long tusks were snapping so you could hear them ever so far. The corn pen was about ten feet high and very small—just four rails square. When filled with corn it was pretty secure, but after the corn had been taken out it was quite shaky. With all of us on one side it jiggled and shook, and our side seemed every moment about to fall down into the midst of the javelinas.

I noticed a most remarkable thing. Five or six of the little wretches would run off into the thicket and come back with another bunch of twelve or fifteen.

My brother threw his cap down amongst them and they simply riddled it. And I'm sure if one of us had fallen he would have met the same fate. I think we must have been there on that tilting rail pen for hours before the people came to our rescue. We screamed and holloed and yelled, and finally the two Laxson boys heard us. They looked out and saw the whole place for two hundred yards around black with the little beasts. The two boys, Johnny and Holly Laxson, came out with their pistols and the javelinas charged them. There happened to be a tree nearby which had been cut down. They sought refuge in the top branches and began shooting. It went on for hours and finally, after they had killed more than a hundred, the others gave up and disappeared into the brush. Where all of them could have come from has always been a mystery to us, but they gathered and gathered the way blackbirds gather sometimes. I think there were several hundred. This episode taught us not to take the dogs to school any more; but still I've known them to attack people who had no dogs with them.

Our friend Captain Wallace had at least one encounter with our teachers. Mother's sister, Aunt Jane Calhoun, lived with Uncle Cal about ten miles from us on the road to San Antonio where we did our shopping. On one occasion when Cap was with us we stopped there to spend the night with our relatives. We found a young lady school teacher had persuaded Aunt Jane to take her to board. She was one of those young squirts who think they know more than anyone else ever knew before, and she simply monopolized the conversation. No one else could say anything and we had her opinion on every subject. When our crowd came in, Aunt Jane was put out some as to what to cook for the midday meal, so she had ham and fried eggs of which there was always plenty on a farm or ranch. The young lady kept on expressing her opinion of what people should or shouldn't do. "Now," she said, "the idea of civilized people having eggs for dinner!"

Cap Wallace stood it as long as he could. Then he gave her one of those keen looks for which he was noted and said, "Young lady, I've seen wilder heifers than you milked in a gourd."

I've often wondered what connection milking heifers in a gourd had with frying eggs for dinner. Anyway the remark had the desired effect and the young lady applied herself to her dinner without any more objections.

THIEVES AND KILLERS

THERE WAS ONE TROUBLE we had in those early days that I could tell a lot about—and that was desperadoes. They got worse and worse as time went on, too, and gave our family its full share of trouble and suffering.

My first experience with such men was not so alarming. It happened when I was still a very little girl. Three very nice, gentlemanly young fellows came to our house and asked Father if he objected to their camping a while in the large oak and mesquite thicket near the back of our house, and if they could water their horses at our well. Father said, "I have no objection—help yourselves."

They were heavily armed and very secretive about their movements. It seemed a little strange to us when they asked Father not to let anyone know they were there, but at that time there were officers about hunting down criminals and we thought they were probably Texas Rangers. The officers used such methods for searching out lawbreakers, murderers and such, so we asked no questions, divulged no secrets, and felt quite safe from marauding Indians and cattle thieves while they were there.

Father told them of the trouble we had been having with the horse and cattle thieves who had begun to molest people, coming in and shooting up everything they could see. One of the men told us if we saw anything more of such rascals we should let them know and they would mix it with them. Then we were sure they were officers of the law. They were very polite and nice; they would come to the house at night to talk politics and the latest news. Once they asked if we had

Sam Bass as Aunt Fan may have known him (University of Texas at Austin, Eugene C. Barker Texas History Center).

heard anything about Joe Collins and Sam Bass. Dad said he had heard of them. One of them said to Father, "I don't suppose Collins and Sam Bass are much good, but don't you think a lot has been said about them that isn't true?"

Father, who never spoke evil of anyone, said, "I pay very little attention to rumors, myself."

Mother baked biscuits and sent them out to their camp, and saw to it that they had milk, butter, and anything she cooked for the family. She knew those poor fellows couldn't cook anything even if they had anything to cook with (which they hadn't) and all the time she was thinking they perhaps were our dearly loved Texas Rangers. She used to say, "Those are sure nice boys."

The day came for them to move on, and they came over to thank us and bid us goodbye. We were all very sad to see our protectors move away, and they said our kindness to them had helped them more than we could know, that they hoped some day they could do something for the family.

Then the great surprise came off. They said they were Frank James, Joe Collins, and Sam Bass, and they hoped we wouldn't report them until they had time to get out of the country. We didn't—and couldn't have if we had wanted to, for there was no one to report them to.

Mother said Sam Bass had the smallest foot and the nicest hands she had ever seen on a man.

Not a great while later Sam Bass was killed at Round Rock, Texas, and soon after that Joe Collins was also killed after robbing a train. I've heard that Frank James changed his name and lived to be an honest man. I don't know about that, but I do know that a few years after leaving his camp at our place he came back to that part of the country. By this time the neighborhood was beginning to be settled up and he stayed with Jesse Laxson. After he was gone, we children and the Laxson youngsters were out hunting with our dogs. The dogs ran a rabbit into the hollow of an old oak tree near their field. We couldn't reach it with our hands—it was too far back in the hollow—so we got a switch and twisted the rabbit out. And with the rabbit out came a package of silver dollars all done up in a roll the way banks handle them. We tore up the earth for yards around but could never dig up any more. Evidently what we found was put there by some of the train robbers.

Frank James, at the time he was visiting the Laxson family, went by the name of Frank Porter, and no one knew outside of our two families that he was Frank James. One might think from the way I am writing that our family was too friendly with some of those desperadoes, but we were decidedly on the other side.

The fact is we had a great deal of trouble with the outlaws, who got very bad in the seventies. They would run through the country, two or three together, and shoot up the settlements—killing dogs, cows, chickens—shooting at everything in sight. Once they shot Mother's coffee pot full of holes. She was making coffee on an outdoor fire place built under the shade of one of the great live oaks that grew in our yard beside the kitchen. She often cooked outside when it was too warm in the kitchen.

Shooting the coffee pot was quite a tragedy because of the distance we had to travel to get another one.

One other time when they were running through the country old Mrs. Crawford stuck her head out of the window to see what the commotion was, and one of the gang yelled, "Take your damned old gray head out of the window before I shoot it off!" Needless to say, she did, and quick.

When these men were in our vicinity, Mother and we children always made a rush for the log kitchen, which stood several feet back of the house. We would lie flat on the floor and although the bullets would sometimes whang against the walls, they never could penetrate the seasoned logs. It was certainly a case of "rats to their holes" when we heard horses' hoofs pounding the highway. Father and Cap Wallace on one occasion grabbed their guns and exchanged shots with the riders from a fence corner, but the night was so dark they couldn't see well enough to hit anybody.

We lived in mortal terror in those days. It was even worse than when the Indians were so bad. Our men did

Frank James as Fan Bramlette knew him (Western History Collection, University of Oklahoma).

everything possible to rid the country of these pests, but they would never come out in the open, preferring to sneak in under cover.

One time our boys did get their chance. The thieves came in and gathered up quite a bunch of horses which they meant to drive out of the country. A band of our men quickly gathered, got on their trail, and on the second day out discovered them camped and fixing their supper on the campfire. The men made a rush on them, shooting them up. They killed one, wounded another, and captured three more. The three captured were taken to San Antonio where they were sentenced to the pen for a number of years.

One of the three after entering the pen refused to comply with any orders given and positively refused to do any work. The prison officials thought they knew how to handle this man, who was known as Harelip. They put him in some kind of tank and started letting the water in, telling him to pump it out with a pump they had installed. The water got higher and higher in the tank, but still he didn't pump, thinking, I suppose, that they would relent and save him. The man who was watching the procedure finally called to him that he was leaving and he could take his choice—pump or drown. And when they went back a short time later he was drowned.

Another of the deperadoes captured at the same time committed suicide. Those who were not with that outfit grew worse and worse, crying for revenge.

One night when our neighbors, the Speed family, were away, they left their colored hired hand Dick to care for the place, and that same night the desperadoes made a raid. As was their habit, they went tearing by the Speed home, shooting at anything and everything. "Nigger Dick," who was sleeping in the wagon out in the yard, awoke and jumped up to see what was going on, and they began shooting all around him. They shot holes in the wagon, and would have shot holes in Dick, for he had a light-colored shirt on, but he tore the shirt off, escaped from the wagon, concealed himself in the brush, and lived to tell the tale.

Those were terrible times. Such nights of horror as we

had, even the children lying awake, not knowing what terrible things might happen before morning. Our clan was holding meetings at different places at night, talking over plans, and while the meetings were going on we at home listened and waited with fear and trembling. We always thought perhaps the desperadoes had an inkling of where the gatherings were being held and, being in the majority, might attack and annihilate our men.

The thieves were particularly angry with the Kercheville boys, Dick, Asa, and Mack, who had bought my Uncle Wynn Haynes's place after Uncle was elected county surveyor and moved to Friotown. The boys had given evidence against one of the gang who had been arrested and tried for horse stealing, and of course their lives were in danger.

Our household was greatly concerned over this, for the Kercheville boys were almost like brothers to us. Our mother mothered them just as if they were her own—she even saw that their clothes were kept clean and ready for them, though she could never understand why they had to have so many white shirts with stiff fronts (which the men wore altogether in those times) for her to iron. She often took a hand in the ironing, for the Mexican women weren't so good at ironing white shirts, especially the ones with stiff or pleated bosoms. When any of the Kercheville boys were ill, she had them brought to the house and kept them until they recuperated. I remember once she nursed Dick through a severe spell of typhoid fever that lasted for a couple of months.

About the time we were being drowned out on the San Miguel a new family named Johnson moved into our neighborhood. They had a young daughter named Bettie and a son Roland who played the violin quite well. They came to our house quite often and were welcome guests—especially Roland, for we young ones all loved to dance and got much fun and enjoyment out of Roland's music. Bettie we all considered a very pretty and attractive girl.

The Kercheville boys, not having good drinking water on their place, hauled their supply as many others did from the Bramlette well. We had the best water in the country. On

Young men of Frio County—Mack Kercheville, lower right (Courtesy of F. M. Kercheville).

one occasion when the boys came to the well for water Bettie was at our house. Mother asked my sister and me to take the water bucket to the well and get some water while the boys were there to draw it for us. Bettie said she would help us carry the water—and that was how Bettie met Dick Kercheville. Dick was so infatuated that he decided to accompany us to the house and stay for a short time, which short time ended when Dad said "Lights out!" Dick, of course, accompanied Bettie home, and in a few months there was a wedding at the Johnson house. To help out with the festivities there was also a dance at the Bramlettes' house which lasted until the wee small hours.

I often spent several days at a time with Bettie and Dick, and many a night the three of us lay awake and watched as the desperadoes waylaid the house, trying to get a shot at the Kercheville boys, whom they hated with a vengeance. One night I remember distinctly we watched through the cracks of the log house, keeping our eyes on a chaparral thicket nearby. The moon was shining brightly and we could easily distinguish figures coming occasionally out of the brush to look about before disappearing again. This went on far into the night. I asked Dick why he didn't shoot at them. He said, "No, wait until they make the first attempt." This was very logical, for as long as they didn't molest us, we were safe; but if we started something we didn't know where we would be, for only Dick was at home that night and we didn't know how many outlaws there were. We believed they were waylaying for Mack and Asa, who were out that evening helping to hold a herd of cattle for a nearby ranchman, or else they were in hopes Dick would show himself outside the house so they could get a shot at him.

On several occasions they tried to ambush the Kercheville boys, and finally did get Mack. It was not long after the episode of which I have just written. The whole countryside was in a flurry of excitement—everyone up in arms and vowing vengeance—when the terrible news came that Mack Kercheville and Ed Grumbles had been murdered while they were asleep. They had been employed by Mr. Johnson (no relation to Bettie Kercheville) to bring a herd of cattle from Mexico back to the Johnson ranch. He had outfitted his men with chuck wagon, horses, and everything else they needed, and had put Grumbles, Kercheville, and another American named Nath Cude in charge of the outfit, which included a Negro cook and two Mexicans. They left early one morning, traveled that day and the next and set up their last camp on the evening of the second day out. The date was March 1, 1881. It was a beautiful moonlight night and all the boys sat up late singing, as cowboys loved to do. Ed and Mack even had a wrestling match before they retired.

They finally went to bed about eleven. All seemed so peaceful and quiet they never had a hint that everything was not as it should be, but a few hours later, when they were all sound asleep, they were suddenly jarred into consciousness by a volley of rifle firing right in the midst of the camp. The treacherous devils had crawled into the midst of the sleeping men and shot Ed through the heart. He died with his pistol in his hand. Mack was shot through the stomach. He crawled a few feet and collapsed. The Negro jumped up and ran, and he too was shot dead in his tracks. One of the Mexicans disappeared and was never heard of again; and it was believed that he was a hired spy for the murderers.

Whoever did the killing must have known exactly where the men were sleeping, for Nath Cude was lying between Mack and Ed, and they reached over him to shoot one of the boys they wanted. Cude and the other Mexican were the only ones left. They took Mack, who was suffering terribly, put him on a bed in the chuck wagon, and started for Fort Ewell, which was not far from where this happened, but they had gone only a short distance when he passed on. Seeing that he was dead, they returned to the camp where they had left the other two dead men and buried them there as best they could. Then they gathered as many of the horses as they could find and came back home to report the terrible tragedy. We could hardly bear to think how those two fine men had been murdered by the low-down, thieving devils, but what could be done about it? We had McNelly's Texas Rangers come out, thinking they could find some solution, but to no avail. Everyone felt sure who the guilty parties were, but could prove nothing.

I believe Dick Kercheville was one of the bravest men I ever knew, as well as one of the handsomest and finest looking. I often think of something my brother-in-law Henry Leuthy told us just after Mack was murdered. Henry and Dick were out riding the range when they met three of the murder suspects. Since they were three to two, I suppose they thought they could run something over Dick. So they drew up and one of them, the very one Dick suspected of being the ringleader, said to him, "I hear you accuse me of being implicated in killing your brother."

Dick answered, "Yes, and I still believe it, and if I was sure, I'd shoot a hole through you that your two charming companions could see daylight through." His forty-five wasn't far from his hand and he was still wearing that little smile which was characteristic of him at all times—so much so that you never could tell when he was angry.

The desperado wasn't so bad as he wished to be considered and he said, "I only wanted to set you straight and let you know I had nothing to do with it."

Dick told him he had better beat it before he forgot himself and shot him anyway, and the men lost no time in doing as they were bidden.

Eventually time and McNelly's Rangers made our country more civilized, but it took us many a long day to get over being nervous. I remember one evening, some time after dark, several horsemen rode up to our house and holloed. Father, not knowing who they might be, took his Winchester to the door and called to them that if they wanted to see him they could come to the door, but to be sure they were not armed. Father was cautious because the desperadoes had been trying to get him too. It turned out that our visitor was none other than Captain McNelly himself. He gave his pistols to one of his men and came to the door, where he told Father that he had been sent to him by a neutral friend. He wanted some place to camp where there was water for his horses and

Texas Rangers, Company C—the unit which came to Frio County in 1874 (Western History Collections, University of Oklahoma).

had been told about our well. Of course everyone knew of our inexhaustible supply of good water where such wells were few and far between, and it seemed there was always somebody, good or bad, camping in our pasture. Dad naturally consented very readily to the Captain's request to stay there, and immediately the family felt a good deal more comfortable.

I think the Rangers were there for several weeks. They had two or three shooting scrapes, made a lot of arrests, and scared the renegades so badly that we didn't hear much of them after that. People began to breathe easier and things got back to normal.

We all would swear by the Rangers and had an idea that they could whip the whole United States Army if it came to a showdown, and I remember how Father and some of the others hated it when McNelly resigned, saying that they would never get another man like him. They gave him full credit for putting down the thieves and desperadoes.

I could give the names of every one of those rustlers, but all of them have children, grandchildren, and all kinds of relatives who I doubt ever have known that their forefathers were such men as they were. They are good citizens and in some cases have married into fine families, and I don't think I'd want to run the risk of getting them or myself into trouble. Besides, there was a perfect nest of people that harbored the outlaws, but we only suspected them and had no positive evidence.

One other tragedy we had in our vicinity was the killing of Green Ridgeway at a dance at Jesse Laxson's. When folks had dances in those days everybody went, since entertainments were very scarce. They would get into their Studebaker wagons or spring wagons and take the entire family, young children, babies, and all. The hostess always prepared a place for the babies to sleep while the mothers and fathers danced.

You might think family troubles would keep people away, but they didn't. There were "hard feelings" between the Laxsons and the McCoys on one side, and the Ridgeways,

Gardiners, and their friends on the other, and strange to say it never seemed to matter who had the dance, picnic, or other gathering—they all attended, whether friend or foe. And so Green Ridgeway showed up at Jesse Laxson's dance as a matter of course.

The guests began gathering at an early hour, as usual. The hostess had the coffee on boiling, and the cookies and cake were ready. Always cake and coffee were served at those gatherings. After the dancing had been going on for some time, Holly Laxson and Green Ridgeway had an altercation over whether or not Holly's wife should dance with Ridgeway. Knowing how matters stood, Ridgeway seemingly would have been wary about asking the wife of one of the other faction to dance, but he asked her for three or four dances in succession. The last time he tried it Holly was sitting beside his wife when Ridgeway came up and said "This is our dance," and started to pull her out onto the floor. Holly said, "I'll be damned if she dances with you any more," and got up and pushed him back. He was trying to push him out of the door when Holly's wife, his mother, and some of the others caught him and pushed him back into his seat, holding him there while Ridgeway went out the door.

They had built a big fire out in the yard and several of Ridgeway's friends were standing around it. Jim McCoy, who was related to the Laxsons, was also there. After a while, when they thought the row was over, the folks in the house turned Holly loose and he and his brother Johnny joined the crowd of men outside. We children were playing around in the yard and had gone to the well to get some water when a boy came to us and told us we had better get back to the house—there was going to be a shooting scrape there in a few minutes. We started back and had got as far as the kitchen in the rear of the house when the shooting began. Three shots were fired in rapid succession, and I remember looking towards the fire and seeing a man sinking slowly down. A woman with a red coat on was going down with him. I ducked behind the big stove in the kitchen, frightened stiff. When I finally made up my mind to come out and go to the house, they had picked up Ridgeway's body and put it on a blanket in front of the fire.

Holly had gone outside, it was said, and was standing by the fire when Ridgeway started to draw his pistol, which he had got hold of in some way after leaving the house. McCoy, seeing him, said, "Don't do it, Green," but it seemed that Green proceeded to pull his gun and McCoy, who was much quicker, shot him before he could fire. I suppose Mrs. Ridgeway, fearing there would be a fight outside, had followed her husband out and tried to catch him as he fell. McCoy shot him twice, and he died instantly. As soon as it was over, McCoy got on his horse and rode away.

Mr. Laxson, Holly's father, told Ridgeway's friends to take him away so they put him into his wagon and took him to his home. All the other folks left the Laxson house after having their refreshments.

McCoy was tried for the killing and came clear, but was hanged not long after for another murder committed near San Antonio. Jim was what one might call a "killer," but was never mixed up with the cattle and horse thievery.

There were others like that. There was always a mistaken idea in after years, in the minds of people who did not know the particulars, about the Allee boys, Alfred and Alonzo. They were as honest as they made them, but unfortunately got involved in several killing scrapes, and later on people mistakenly mixed them up with the common desperadoes and rustlers. Like many other Texans in those days they were pretty handy with their pistols, and I have a faint remembrance of two or three shooting frays they were in. One in particular comes to my mind. It seems that Alfred was drinking in some saloon in Pleasanton (near which they lived) when a big black Negro came in, one with whom Allee had had an altercation before. This Negro saw Alfred talking to some friends near the bar, leaned over and put his arm around Allee's shoulder, and said, "Belly up, Allee, and have one on me." Believing, like many other Southern men, that the Negro should keep his place and respect the white folks, Alfred pushed him back. This made him angry; he started to

Alfred Allee, Texas Ranger famous in his day (University of Texas at Austin, Eugene C. Barker Texas History Center).

fight; and Alfred shot him. He must have been intoxicated or he wouldn't have tried to be so intimate.

Allee was tried before a Texas jury and needless to say he came clear.

Alfred was married when I first met him, and I never knew him as well as I did Alonzo, though I have danced with him when we attended the dances at Pearsall. I remember that Alonzo once gave me a beautiful cameo ring for a Christmas present and that I was his partner at many dances. There were never any nicer boys than the Allees.

GROWING UP

By the time we were thirteen or fourteen years old my sister and I began to think we were almost young ladies. We began to "primp up," wear bustles made out of newspapers, and notice the boys. And of course we tried to be beautiful. In those days toilet articles and beautifiers of any kind were impossible for us to get, so we had to improvise. When preparing for parties we would get Father's branding iron and take the brand part off, leaving a straight rod of iron about the size we wanted our curls to be. We would heat the iron in the stove and use it for curling our hair. With a scrap of red cheesecloth for rouge and prepared chalk for powder, we considered we had got ourselves up in pretty good style.

We were living in another house now. Shortly after the killing of Ridgeway, Father bought Jesse Laxson's ranch and moved the school house, where we went to school, up near the old Laxson home. There was a public school by this time at "Longview" (named for James Long, who had a large ranch there). When the building was moved, Father added to it until we had a fairly nice home, and then he and Mother went to San Antonio and bought furniture—bedroom sets, bureaus, wardrobes, tables, and rocking chairs. We girls were very proud of them and felt we were making progress. At that time no one had living-room suites out where we were.

We often had company. On our trips to San Antonio Dad and Mother would bring back some of their friends' children to spend a week or two on the ranch. I remember one boy about twelve years old, Louis Hader, who liked my sister but wasn't much taken with me—I suppose because I regarded

A relic of old Friotown (University of Texas Institute of Texan Cultures).

him as an infant and Sister treated him differently. He would say, "Now just watch Miss Fan stand before the mirror and twist off and look back at it while Miss Allie is doing all the work." I must have been an awful upstart of a brat.

Our new house was very near the McMahons, and Sallie McMahon and I were chums. Hardly a day passed that we were not together, and often we would spend the nights with each other. The McMahons had quite a bunch of hogs which they fed with the skimmed milk after it had soured. Some one told Sallie and me that if we would soak cloths in very sour buttermilk, double them several times, and make masks of them, they would make our complexions very beautiful. We were reaching the age when we were thinking we would like to be beautiful, and we decided to try it out. We got our masks ready, soaked them in buttermilk so sour you could smell it a mile off, and had just put them in place when Sallie's mother asked us to go out to the cow pen and let the calves out. The hogs were always fed at the cow pen, so when Sallie and I opened the gate the hogs, smelling the sour milk on our faces, thought we had come to feed them and made a rush at us, squealing at the top of their voices. We made tracks to the house as hard as we could run, the hogs just a step behind us all the way. They chased us through the yard gate, which fortunately we had left open, and clear up onto the porch. We were two scared gals, for I don't know what they would have done to us if they had caught us—torn us to pieces, probably.

Sallie had a pony and saddle—a side saddle, of course. We would have been ostracized if we had ridden the way girls do these days. Naturally we wanted to ride too, so Father gave my sister and me a beautiful pony each and he and Mother went to San Antonio to buy us each a nice saddle. Then Sallie, Sister, and I had a lot of fun horseback riding. We all, of course, had learned to ride like the "old cowhand" in the song almost before we "learned to stand," but always on cowboys' saddles, or bareback. I could stand on my horse's back while he was in a gallop, but I'm not going to tell how many falls I got before I learned the trick.

We would often ride our ponies over to visit a new family who had bought a large ranch and built a nice home over on the San Miguel. They had a very charming daughter about our age and an awfully good-looking son a little older than I who afterwards became my first beau. I don't yet know which of the two was the greater attraction. I am inclined to think it was the brother, but we thought a mighty lot of the charming sister.

I thought Maggie, the new girl, very beautiful—in fact, one of the most perfectly lovely persons I ever saw. I thought about it a great deal, wondering why some girls were endowed with all the gifts and why I didn't have some of them. One day I stood before the mirror taking inventory of myself, wondering if there was any way to improve my appearance. "Now," I said to myself, "My hair is exactly like Maggie's; my complexion about the same; my eyes the same color; face not bad looking. Maybe there is a chance to do something to make me more attractive." But what to do I hardly knew. Finally, after looking at myself from all angles, I thought, "Maybe I should try to look like Maggie." So I began to copy first one, then another of her little mannerisms. She always wore a long, flying veil when riding, pinned around her riding hat across her forehead. I got me a long veil and pinned it likewise and tried to smile and hold my head like Maggie. Imagine my delight one day when one of my boy cousins said, "Fan, you look just like Maggie. . . ."

We had already begun going to dances and dancing with the young men, though only about fourteen and fifteen years of age. In those days girls thought they were grown up earlier than they do now. When I was fifteen I had my first beau— none other than the handsome brother of the attractive Maggie. I can remember it so distinctly because I was all excited about it, and also because I was getting one on Sallie. There was a dance at the home of Bud Thompson, a near neighbor of Dick and Bettie, so I could go from there. Lem Kercheville accompanied me to the dance. After spending a delightful evening dancing to the music of Jim Sadler's and Roland Johnson's violins, we heard the strains of "Home, Sweet Home." Evart asked me to dance it with him, and afterward said, "Now you have danced 'Home, Sweet Home' with me, I'm supposed to accompany you home." I was terribly embarrassed and hardly knew what to say. Lem, who heard him, said, "Of course, come on Evart and go along." I suppose I must have been one of the silliest kids, for I don't believe I said three words all the way. To make matters worse, Evart said, "What on earth is the matter? Have you forgotten how to talk?" And though I was very much thrilled at having him see me home, I knew I had made a dummy of myself and thought, "I'm never, never going anywhere with another boy."

I soon got over that idea, for there was going to be a picnic and barbecue on the Fourth of July and Evart dispatched a boy with a note asking if he might come by to accompany me to the barbecue. He asked if I'd prefer going in the buggy or on horseback, and wanted me to let him know by the bearer. I replied that I would prefer going on horseback, thinking to impress him with my superior horsemanship. When the happy day arrived, my sister (who was going with Lem) and I were arrayed in our new black riding habits and riding hats, and thought we were startlingly beautiful. Evidently the boys thought something like that too, for they hardly left our sides during the whole day. I had been somewhat disturbed a few days before by hearing that Sallie had been spending several days with Maggie and had been seen out driving with Evart, but now I felt better.

By this time I was beginning to think quite a lot about Evart and to plan for the next time he would ask me for a date, but the next time I went out with him was quite a while later. There was going to be a dance over in the Obitz settlement near the little town of Moore. Maggie sent a note to Sister, Sallie and me asking us to come to her house early in the afternoon the day of the dance and we would all go from there. We, of course, were delighted to do so, and I began to wonder which one Evart would ask to go with—Sallie or me. We all gathered at their home—Asa Kercheville, Lem Kercheville, Wylie Mangum, Sallie, and I. After dinner we began getting ready to go to the dance, which was only four or five miles away. The boys saddled and led out their horses to where ours were, and I think every one of us girls was in a flutter wondering which boy was going with which girl. When we all started out to the gate where the horses were tied my heart almost stopped, for there right beside Sallie's horse stood Evart, and I thought, "Gee, Sallie is going to score on me this time." But imagine my delight when he deliberately untied his pony, led it over to where mine was, and said, "Come on, Fan, it's time we were riding." I took one triumphant glance at Sallie, who was looking somewhat crestfallen, and skipped up to my horse. Evart put his hand out, I put the tip of my toe in his hand, and bounced happily up. Sallie teamed up with Wylie Mangum, Sister with Lem, and Maggie with Asa. We all had a grand time at the dance and spent the next day with Maggie. Evart and I came to somewhat of an understanding that night going home from the party—at least he asked me to be his girl and I said I would. A short time after that he went away to college and asked if he might write to me. Of course I was delighted, and said so.

That was the last I saw of Evart for a long time. He was very popular with the girls; they fell over themselves to get a dance with him or to be in his presence. So I was determined that he shouldn't think I was running after him and was more determined than ever when his sister remarked in my presence that all the girls where he was attending school were crazy about him and that from what she could hear he was very much attracted towards a girl there. All this was, I suppose, for Sallie's and my benefit. Anyway when a letter came for me after what I thought too long a time, I, like a little idiot, took it over to Sallie's house just to show her I had a letter from him and she hadn't. As it was pretty sweet, I let her read it and remarked that I supposed he was going with the girl Maggie had told us about. Sallie said, "I know he is," and pretended that Maggie had told her other things about it. She said, "He's just trying to make a fool out of both of us, and wouldn't it be fun just to write and tell him you had showed his letter to everybody and you all had a big laugh over it?" I thought that would be quite cute and would show him here was one that wasn't crazy about him. So I sent him the nastiest letter and, as I found out later, without any cause. I little thought at the time that I was being "played for a sucker." He wrote back, and I, still being smarty, sent his letter back unopened while Sallie enjoyed every minute of the affair, for of course I had to tell her everything even though I knew she was crazy about Evart herself.

Of course I never heard from Evart again, but the days went on, and it was almost time for him to be home again for vacation. I thought perhaps he would bury the hatchet and start over. During this time another new family had moved into the settlement—the Iveys from, I think, Caldwell County. They had two boys, Otis and Ed. The Kercheville boys, the Ivey boys, and a few others decided on having a tournament. Evart came home just in time to practice for it.

When I first saw him after his return from school, he was all diked out in his gray uniform with black stripes down the legs, brass buttons, and a coat which fitted as if he had on a corset. He was all reared back like a major general. Gosh, but he looked handsome! I thought to myself, "Now he thinks the girls are all daffy about him. I'm glad I wrote to him like I did." I pretended not to see him, but toward the end of the dance he came and asked me to dance. I said, "No, thank you"—and dying to make up with him all the time. Now if anybody can tell me why people make such fools of themselves, I'd like to know the reason.

Before long it was time for the tournament. Not many people today know how they played in those tournaments, and for the benefit of those who never had the pleasure of seeing one, I shall describe the procedure. First they put up several long poles with an arm fastened to the top and extending out over the track where the horses run. On these arms were strung rings, and the men on horseback would ride past the poles at a gallop and try to catch those rings on long spears with metal points. The one that got the most rings was the winner and received a crown made beautiful with flowers, tinsel, etc. The boy who got next to the most won the first wreath, and so on down. The boys were supposed to crown girls they liked best and take them to the dance which was customarily held after the tournament.

Now to go back to our tournament—when the day came the whole countryside gathered to see it, especially the gentry. In rode the eight boys, all in black suits with wide red sashes over one shoulder and tied under the opposite arm. Those riding were Ed and Otis Ivey, Asa and Lem Kercheville, Wylie Mangum, Evart, and two others whom I can't remember. They certainly looked gay and festive with their red sashes and caps.

The tournament lasted about three quarters of an hour. I think they ran through six times each. When it ended Evart had won the crown, Ed Ivey the first wreath, and other boys, in whom I was not so much interested, the rest. I knew Ed would choose Maggie to wear his wreath, but I wondered about Evart. Of course, after our falling out, I could hardly hope that he would choose me, but still, I thought, miracles do happen. I was pretty close to Maggie and Sallie (Sallie having been at Maggie's house visiting ever since Evart's return). I had my back turned towards the girls talking to someone behind them, but don't think I didn't know what was going on behind me even though I wouldn't turn around for fear of looking too hopeful! With the ear I had turned in that direction I heard Sallie say, "Oh, thank you!" just as if she didn't know all the time she was going to get it. I then turned around and congratulated her and Maggie, telling them how perfectly grand the crown and wreath were and how pretty they made them look. Evart was standing near. I said, "Hello! So glad you were the lucky one." He came up and shook hands with me, looking as if he wanted to say, "See what you missed by being so smarty." I wasn't so mad at Evart, but knowing that was what Sallie was working for all the time, I felt like pulling her hair off, crown and all, and throwing it in her face. Anyway I never let Evart know that I cared anything about it, and I think that he felt disappointed because I acted so indifferent.

After the crowning of the queen and her attendants, we all went home to wait for the big dance to come off. Though I have always been very keen about taking in all the dances and parties, I some way didn't care whether I went to this dance or not. But for fear people would think I stayed away on account of Sallie's getting the crown, I decided it would be better policy to go. So I did, and believe it or not Evart danced almost every dance with me, to the utter disgust of Sallie. During the whole evening neither he nor I mentioned the tournament or the letters.

Someone must have told my Aunt Sarah about Evart's paying so much attention to me at the dance, for over she came next day in her gig, driving her dun-colored pony, in a mighty huff. She told Mother she thought Evart and I were getting pretty thick and said, "Sis, you'd better nip that in the bud before it goes any further." We had already innocently disobeyed Mother's orders not to go to the dance on account of the death of one of our uncles by marriage in San Antonio a couple of months before. She had given her consent to our going to the tournament but told us to come home when it was over and not to go to the dance. This didn't suit the girls and boys, and after the performance they persuaded us to let one of them ride over and ask Mother if we might stay. Mother told him "Certainly not!" and sent word for us to come home immediately. The boy came back and said she had given her consent to our staying. When we got back next day, she met us at the door and of all the talking I ever heard, I think that eclipsed everything. In those days children had to obey their parents, and it seemed Mother was the strictest of them all—to "sauce" her was unheard of. I did manage to tell her that Uncle John Jordan was as dead as he'd ever be, and I thought she was going to murder me. Then next day came Aunt Sarah's visit, and that added fuel to the fire.

Acting somewhat, I think, on Aunt Sarah's advice, Mother told me a few days later she thought it would be a good idea for me to go to Friotown, where Uncle Wynn and Aunt Sarah Ann lived, and start school. The beginning of the next session was only a couple of months off. Of course the idea of going some place appealed to me.

A few days later my uncle and aunt came down to spend

a couple of weeks with Mother and Father, as was a habit with them. Mother and my aunt talked it over and decided that I should go back with them when they went. They got busy making my clothes ready, and when the time came they hustled me and my bags into the hack, and off to Friotown we went.

Had Mother only known it, this was a case of out of the frying pan into the fire, for I had no more than landed when I was introduced by my aunt to a very charming girl named Mary Little who had a very nice-looking brother, Dave. From our first meeting Dave and I liked each other very much and began going together right away. My aunt didn't object since the Littles were one of the best families in Friotown. We went together the whole time I was there and that made it very pleasant for me because I got to attend many parties and dances to which I could not otherwise have gone.

I still couldn't forget my first beau and wondered about him a lot, but it was many years before I saw him again. When vacation time came and I went home, he had gone away and did not come back while I was there. I finally ceased to think of him, but years later, after we were both married, I happened to meet him again. Strange to say, it was at the home of my Aunt Sarah Thomas. He was president of a nearby bank where Aunt did her banking and had come to see her on business. When he walked into the house, my aunt said, "Fan, this is Evart. Do you remember him?" I said, "Oh, yes! he's the boy I was once so crazy about." He quickly replied, "I never saw you standing on your head boring any holes in the ground about me." I thought, no, you didn't but that's no sign I didn't almost do it. I had a mind to say to Aunt Sarah, "Things might have been different if you hadn't nipped it in the bud," but I didn't. And that is the last I ever saw of Evart.

I had been in Friotown only a short time when I met Simeon Williams, who was still in school, and we became fast friends. I asked her what she studied and asked her to show me her school books. She began pulling out philosophy books, and a lot of others I had heard Father and Mother discuss but had never studied. I thought, Great Heavens! I don't even know how to start studying those things. She was a very sweet, understanding girl, so I confided in her my inability to cope with the situation. I told her I wasn't going to school—would run away and go back home before I'd be embarrassed by not being in the class my age called for. Simeon said, "Oh, no, let's get to work. It's still some time before school starts." So we took her school books and began studying, and I don't believe I ever worked so hard in my life. Simeon stayed right with me, and when school began I at least knew something about what the books meant. With her help every night, at either her house or mine, I managed to stay in the class and answer some, at least, of the questions. Mrs. Coats, our teacher, was very kind and helped us along, but I don't think she was very much impressed with my superior knowledge.

The Slaughter family, long-time friends of my father, were living at or near Friotown. Among them was Uncle Ben Slaughter, whose sons Billy and Charley had fought with Dad in the Confederacy. Father, being an officer and having some influence, got the two boys furloughed and sent home, as they had both contracted malaria in the swamps of Louisiana. Long after the war when Dad asked Uncle Ben if he ever prayed, he replied, "I promised the Lord if he would send my boys back from the war I would never ask for anything else. I wouldn't want to break my promise."

Uncle Billy had six girls, all at home except his oldest daughter Amanda, who had married a man named Taylor. As soon as the girls knew I was there, they called on me, and I became good friends with all of them. Fannie and Artie were near my age and of course we were together most, but I often spent the weekends with all of them at the Slaughter home. The girls had their own governess and music teacher, so we were not together in the school room, but during the time I was at my uncle's my brother Pat came to stay with Grandfather and Grandmother Slaughter and attend school and we all saw each other quite often, especially at dances.

When I had been in Friotown only a short time the

Slaughter girls complimented me with a dinner dance so that I could meet the young folks of the place. They had a lovely home and everything was beautifully decorated. I remember I had what I thought was a very attractive dress for the occasion. The bodice was of bright red satin; there was a tight, pointed basque, low in the neck, very short sleeves, and a row of tiny red satin buttons down the front set as close together as possible. I had a white swiss skirt with little ruffles to the waist (I had fluted all the ruffles with a fluting machine), red stockings the same shade as the basque, and black slippers. I thought I looked too cute for anything.

And what a wonderful time we did have! Dancing was one of the social graces and we children were so well trained I don't think we could have been beaten anywhere. We had started dancing when we were very small—danced on the road to school—danced while helping with the housework. Every place we went, we went dancing, thanks to Aunt Sarah Ann Haynes who taught us to waltz, schottische, polka, do the highland fling, and all the rest of the dances in vogue in those days. And how we did love a quadrille!

There were quite a number of young girls in Friotown and all very nice people. The town was made up mostly of ranchers, many of them owners of large pastures and large herds—quite wealthy people who sent their children to good schools and colleges and were all, in fact, people of the upper class. I think I can remember most of them. Besides the Slaughter girls there were Mary Little, Simeon Williams, Mollie and Ella Baldwin, Alice Martin, Cora and Lydia Hearne, Jimmie and Kitty Powers, Kate and Annie Hennings, Sallie and Nola Blackaller. These were the ones I knew best and the ones who took part in all the social activities. Besides the few boys who lived in town, there were dozens who came from their ranch homes.

Most of our big dances were in the courthouse where there was an enormous hall with a floor as slick as glass. The orchestra consisted of two violins, a bass viol, and "Nigger Doc" with his immense accordion. I have never seen anything like that accordion before or since. It had big silver bells on top which also played the music. When we were all assembled we could hardly hold our feet till the music began, and the dancing went on until the wee small hours.

The time I spent in Friotown was, I'm sure, the most enjoyable of my entire life.

A while before I went to Friotown my friends the Littles had a terrible tragedy in their lives. They had a lovely daughter named Maggie who had married Harry Graham. There was a beautiful wedding and a dance that lasted all night with everything to make it a grand affair. The morning after the wedding Harry and Maggie started, with several others, for New Mexico, where they planned to live. At this time the Indians were very bad in the western part of Texas and in New Mexico. The wagon train had arrived somewhere near the Pecos River when it was attacked just after stopping to make camp for the night. The teams had just been taken out and unharnessed when a large band of Indians hidden in the nearby brush commenced firing. The folks got under the wagons as the safest place to fight from, and they kept up a resistance for quite a while. Harry was shot in the leg and was bleeding profusely, but worse than that he ran out of ammunition. Not being able to move himself, he asked Maggie to get up in the wagon and bring another Winchester and cartridges to him. She went after them, but just as she bent over the front board of the wagon, the Indians shot her through the head and killed her instantly. The whole outfit was wiped out except Harry Graham, who, when he saw that all the others were dead, managed to pull himself up on one of the horses and miraculously escaped. He made his way to the settlements, reported the tragedy, got help, and went back to the scene of the massacre, where they buried the dead as well as they could. The Indians had burned the wagons and everything else they couldn't carry away, stolen the horses, and got away without being molested. Mrs. Little never got over grieving for her daughter. Years later on the anniversary of the tragedy she would shut herself up in her room and weep all day.

I liked Friotown very much and dreaded the time when I

should have to leave. I wanted to see my parents and the youngsters at home but I knew it was going to be lonely after I had had such a lot of social activity. Uncle Billy Slaughter asked me to stay in his home and share the advantages of school and music with his girls, but I refused. Now here is something I wish the psychologists would explain. There was nothing in the world I should have liked better than to enjoy the privileges of that lovely home and the company of those interesting daughters, to say nothing of the educational advantages I could have had. But I just said, "Thank you, Uncle Billy, I couldn't think of it." I never could understand whether I refused because I expected to be persuaded or because of false pride when all the time I was dying to accept.

About this time the little town of Pearsall was booming, it being on the new I. & G.N. Railway. There were new stores, hotels, schools, churches, and everything it takes to make a booming little city. Many of the merchants and businessmen from Friotown and other places were moving their businesses to Pearsall. It was a lively place and every weekend there would be a dance either at one of the hotels or in the hall which had been built for entertainments. We girls and boys would all get together and go from Friotown to Pearsall to the dances and have a wonderful time.

I remember once when my sister Alice was visiting us at Uncle Wynn Haynes' in Friotown a very popular young man—quite a catch—became interested in her. He had the finest and fastest team of horses in town and a beautiful, silver-tired buggy which glistened in the sunlight until it hurt your eyes. She would look so smug when he drove her by all the other carriages, buggies, and hacks, and I think the other boys felt like committing mayhem.

It wasn't long after this that an election was held to decide if the county seat should be moved to Pearsall, where it would be more centrally located, or remain in Friotown. It was moved to Pearsall, so my Uncles Wynn Haynes and Sam and John Thomas, who were county officers, had to move to the new county seat. Sister and I visited them there often. I remember on one of my visits I met two of Uncle Haynes's cousins from Tennessee—Bob and Alf Taylor, who ran against each other for governor. They were both very nice and interesting.

We always had a joyous time while visiting the Haynes family at Pearsall. All of them were and are musicians, and when at home before they married and scattered out they had a regular family band. Their home was a gathering place for all the young people, and my aunt and uncle were as jolly and seemed to have as much fun as the young people. The Haynes children all seemed more like sisters and brothers than cousins, but a special favorite was Sophia Alice, who was called Dink—I don't know why. She was always full of fun, and still is, and was one of those young girls who would tell us all about her romances. One funny little incident which always amused me greatly happened while Dink was going to high school in Pearsall. She and Ida Slaughter were chums and had got up school-girl cases on the two Woodward brothers, Charley and Ross. One of their tricks was passing notes back and forth in the school room. Ross one time wrote one to Dink and successfully passed it to her. She put it in her school book, and on her way up to ask the teacher something she wanted to know, she dropped it on the floor. Some of the pupils, seeing a note on the floor, picked it up and gave it to the teacher who, after unfolding it and reading it, looked up and asked, "Who is 'Dearest Dinkum?'" Dink was scared stiff and Ida nearly choked with laughter, but no one seemed to know who Dearest Dinkum was.

Dink was always reading, and no matter what she had to do she started at it with a book in her hand. Consequently she thoughtlessly did a lot of funny things. One day my aunt told her to go into the kitchen and put some wood in the stove (we had only wood stoves in those days). Dink, still reading her book, reached down to get the stove hook which she thought she saw on the floor. What she got hold of was the tail of the old cat, who was lying on the floor under the stove with only her tail sticking out. She hauled the old cat up by the tail, not knowing the difference, until the poor animal let out a yell, and this frightened her so that she jumped and turned the pot of boiling coffee over on her feet, not entirely missing the cat. The yelling of the two brought my infuriated aunt into the kitchen. She was already very angry with Dink for something she had done the day before. Sent to grind some coffee and put it in the coffee pot, Dink strolled in, book in hand, ground the coffee, and deliberately poured it into a pot of chicken and dumplings Aunt had on the stove cooking for dinner.

Another time Aunt sent her in to parch some coffee. At that time everybody parched coffee. We put it into a square bread pan and put it into the oven. As it browned on top, we would take it out and stir it, keeping that up until it was thoroughly browned. Dink, book in hand, proceeded to put her coffee into the pan and into the stove to brown, but her coffee happened to be brown beans. She had got into the bean sack instead of the coffee. She never noticed the difference until my aunt, smelling the strange odor, came to see what was going on. Opening the stove, she discovered the scorched frijoles.

PREACHERS, PARTIES
AND
OTHER DIVERSIONS

AFTER LEAVING FRIOTOWN and my school friends I was at first happy over seeing the home folks, but life in the country soon began to seem very humdrum. To break the monotony I resumed my friendship with Annie Long, a girl I had known for years, and we had a lot of fun together. I also found that a family named Cochran had moved into the community while I was away, bringing with them a young daughter about my age whom I liked very much. The three of us made quite a team. We all had brothers nearly our age, and with two other boys, Lem Kercheville and Theodore Pyle, we were always into all the innocent fun and devilment we could think of. Annie's parents were active workers in the Baptist Church and the Baptist people had built a big arbor not very far from the Long home where they held meetings that lasted for two or three weeks. During the protracted meetings I would always stay with Annie and attend.

We were both members of the church, I having joined at the age of eleven, but we youngsters were always so full of mischief that our being members of the church didn't keep us from having all the fun we could get out of it. Once I remember some members of the congregation had brought the preacher a lot of the nicest-looking watermelons I ever saw. They were brought in the morning and lay around the "mourners' bench" on the floor, which was covered with straw. So our bunch began planning how we were going to get some of the preacher's melons. One of the crowd was delegated to go up to the mourners' bench to be prayed for. The others were to sit along the aisle, and the one at the mourner's bench would reach down, while everybody was praying and unable to see him, and start the melons rolling toward the door. The others sitting along the aisle would kick each one along until it got near enough to the door for the ones standing outside to pick it up and put it in the Longs' hack. While the prayer was still going on, we would sneak out to the hack, go out on the road some place with our melons, eat them, and get back before the folks wanted to go home. We actually carried this scheme out, and there were a dozen others that we worked at one time or another. I often wonder why our people didn't get next to some of our capers, but they never did. I suppose they thought we were such good little girls we couldn't be guilty of such deeds; and too, our brothers were with us all the time. I suppose they had no idea the brothers were just as bad as we were, and often put us up to a lot of pranks which otherwise we wouldn't have been into.

There was a young preacher who stayed at the Cochran home and had charge of the little church at Bigfoot—a tall, red-cheeked tenderfoot, very fair and very red-lipped—who took a mighty fancy to me and tried to get me to go with him. I couldn't get rid of him in any way. My crowd got an awful kick out of it and loved to tease me about him, which didn't tend to make me love him any better. He kept on pursuing me, and preached with his eyes always set on me. I finally got so disgusted with him that I took to making faces at him during the sermon and kept it up until finally he got the idea that I didn't want to be bothered with him. He knew all the time that Annie and I were not behaving with the proper decorum in church, but until he found out how I felt about him he seemed to take it all in good humor. However, he let things run along until his time was about up and he wasn't going to stay there any longer. On his last Sunday, after the sermon was over, he said, "There is something I'd like to bring before the congregation. Besides other things of which she has been guilty, Sister Fannie Bramlette has stuck a pin in Sister Wallace."

Sister Wallace was one of those big fat women who laced so tight she looked as if she would burst if you stuck a pin in her. I mentioned this to Annie, so she dared me to try it. I did, and Sister Wallace reported this, and the faces I had been making, to the minister. I can see now that those were terrible things to be guilty of, but we thought them funny at the time.

The preacher had no more than got the words out of his mouth when a friend of the family, a leading member of the Baptist Church, spoke up and said,

"Never mind about that, Brother Morris. This is your last day and we will attend to all the other things later."

I never heard any more about the matter, but imagine my consternation when he made the statement. I made up my mind that we had better confine our activities to other places than the church.

Things were evened up with Mr. Preacher before he left. While he and M. B. Cochran (brother of the Queen, who was a partner in our "carryings-on") were out in the field one day, they found a skunk under some bushes and the preacher exclaimed, "Oh, what a beautiful cat!" The "cat," being frightened, began running, the preacher right behind him. M. B. was hollering, "Catch him, Preacher; catch him!" The man got almost near enough to catch the creature and had bent over to pick him up when he fell back with an awful cry and commenced wallowing on the ground. M. B. doubled up and almost died laughing.

The preacher had a fearful time ridding himself of the perfume. M. B. told me the next time I saw him that he had got revenge for the preacher's attempt to turn me out of the church. Those boys always stuck up for us no matter what we did, though really all we were ever guilty of was some sort of prank done just for the fun of it.

It seemed natural for our bunch to stick together and have nothing to do with the other girls and boys in the community. I suppose we thought we were something extra special because we had all the nicest boys in our crowd, and when new ones came in, we were the first ones they cared to meet. Besides, we thought, weren't our daddies the biggest land owners, and didn't we live in the better houses? Then too, Mother was always very particular about our associations and would never, if she knew it, consent to our going to any parties or dances given by some of the people there. The Southern folks were clannish and seemed to cling to their old traditions.

We had two lovely girlfriends in a nearby family, originally from South Carolina. Their father had lost everything when the slaves were set free and never seemed to "get his foot on the right pedal" after coming to the new country. These girls, not being able to hire their washing done, would wash in the house and hire a Negro woman for twenty-five cents to hang the clothes on the line, saying they would be embarrassed to tears for the neighbors to see them hanging out clothes. It seems funny now, to think how the Southern women felt about those things, but it was certainly not funny at the time.

It was the same about dances. It seemed that Mother objected to most of the places where we wanted to go to dance. Once one of the country families was giving a *big* dance— having a fine dinner, importing musicians from town, and expecting lots of people. My sister, brother and I were dying to go, but we knew there was no earthly use in asking Mother, knowing full well that she would refuse. So we began planning some way to get off to the dance without her knowing about it. First we planned to ask her permission to spend the night out. Sister and I would stay with one of the neighbor girls and Brother would tell Mother he was going out coon hunting. He would get his clothes out of the house and dress, take our saddles out to a nearby thicket, hide our ponies out there early in the evening, and come by for us with the complete equipment later on. However, when we asked Mother if we might spend the night with our girlfriend, she caught on right away and said, "What are you up to? You know Sallie is going to that dance tonight." So that was off. And what next to do? We were determined to go to that dance if it was humanly possible.

Brother said, "I'll get the ponies and take the saddles out to the thicket. You girls dress and put some old clothes over your party dresses—drop your nice shoes out of the bedroom window—sit around with the family until they decide to re- tire—then go to your room and put out the light. Sit very quietly until you think they are asleep—then crawl out the window and meet me where the horses are tied."

Sister and I put on a pretty good show. It was fortunate that we always had our hair combed and our faces powdered. We sat up as long as Father and Mother did so as to give them no room for suspicion. After they went to bed, which wasn't very late, we quietly took off our top dresses, slipped into our party dresses, and crawled through the window. We had al- ready opened it and arranged a box on the outside so we could get down with as little noise as possible. Once outside we picked up our party shoes and made for the thicket where Brother was waiting very impatiently, and we went to the dance, running our horses the six miles we had to go because we were so late getting started.

We had a very nice time, but every little while I'd stop in the middle of my gaiety and wonder if Mother had missed us yet. I kept thinking, wouldn't it be terrible if she should ap- pear in the doorway; for she was a very determined woman and might have followed us. But she didn't—and we danced until long after midnight. All the way home I was shivering in my shoes, sure that Mother would have missed us, but we got back, crawled through the window very silently, and congrat- ulated ourselves that we had "turned the trick."

Early the next morning we found out how deceived we were. Just about daylight we heard an angry voice saying, "Get right out of that bed, and do it in a hurry!" We looked up to see her with a board in her hand, and we thought, "Oh Lord! Now we are in for it." She disappeared into the kitchen and came back with a tea kettle of boiling water. By then we were mostly dressed. She said, "You had better have been up from there or I would have gotten you out mighty quick." We knew that was a bluff, for we were sure she wouldn't have done anything with that hot water, but in those times youngsters were supposed to obey their parents. Mr. Wallace got a big kick out of that, and when I did anything he thought she wouldn't approve of, he would say, "Watch out, Fan. Don't forget Mom and the tea kettle."

In the summer time we always had a crowd of visitors, generally our relatives, especially Aunt Sarah Ann, Uncle Wynn Haynes, and their families. Often Uncle Sam Thomas's family spent part of the summer months, and besides there were visitors from San Antonio. One summer we had Cousin Amanda and Cousin Will Wallingford from Center, Texas, and we were such a jolly set that the young folks from Devine and Moore would often join us. We had a croquet set, big swings put up in the shade of the grand old oak trees, plenty of riding ponies, and everything to add to our enjoyment. We would have as many as fifteen house guests at a time. I often wonder how Mother managed to feed so many people, for we never had a servant who could cook—they were all Mexicans and not at all well trained. I also wonder how she could find places for so many to sleep; but manage she did, and I suppose made everybody comfortable, for they never failed to come back.

We had a lot of fun at those swings on nice moonlight nights and I believe the moon shone brighter there than anywhere else. We would go out and sit on the benches and in the swings and tell stories and sing and have a wonderful time. The porch would be full of neighbors, who never failed to put in an appearance. Our porch was about forty feet long by ten wide and we had room for all. Sometimes we would get too noisy and Dad would say, "Lights out!" which always meant for us to break up and go to bed. After we girls got older, our house was always a gathering place for all the young folks in the neighborhood.

Christmas and the Fourth of July were always the gala

times. Mother began getting things fixed far ahead of time. The house had to be thoroughly cleaned, windows, walls, floors. Curtains had to be washed and rehung—the yard cleaned (for a hundred yards around, I thought at the time)— and then, when everything was about shipshape, the grand cooking came off. There were hams to be baked or boiled, chickens and turkeys (which had been penned up and fed for the occasion) to be cooked, pies and cakes to be baked, light bread to be made. Mother had the men swing a two-foot shelf up in the kitchen clear across the width of the room, and the day before Christmas we began filling it up with cakes and pies, generally sitting up to all hours before we were through. When we were finished, that long shelf would be full. I think we had every kind of pie and cake that was known at that time and two ten-gallon lard cans filled with light bread.

Early Christmas morning the fun would begin. Our relatives who lived at a distance always arrived the day before, and those who were living near got there by daylight. The festivities began with an eggnog early in the morning which the others concocted while Mother was busy getting the turkeys and chickens cooked. Breakfast was next in order after the eggnog—sausage, hot biscuits, preserves, and butter— while the youngsters were making music with the drums, bugles and whistles they had found in their stockings. Later the neighbors would begin to gather in to help celebrate, and many times we had as many as thirty people to dinner. Often when the weather was good (which it generally was) we would make a long table out of doors by fitting three twelve-inch planks on top of two-by-fours nailed to four standards. In that way we would have plenty of room at the one table; otherwise we had to have tables all over the house.

Once or twice I spent Christmas away from home. I remember when sister Canby Alice and I were around sixteen and seventeen years of age there was going to be an unusually gay time in Pearsall—balls, parties, and all kinds of amusements—and of course, since we had so many friends there and at Friotown, we were invited to come. Our friends the Hearn girls at the Hearn Hotel asked us to stay with them, and as our chances for such enjoyment were not many, we made great preparations.

Mr. Davis had a dry goods store in Devine and kept a very nice stock of materials for dresses, so Sister and I got on our ponies and rode over. Dad had an account at Davis's store, as he had in all the others, and never curbed our spending or said one word, no matter what we bought, and it never occurred to us that things had to be paid for. I really don't think we would have known how to buy with cash, for all the stockmen paid their bills once a year.

Sister and I decided that we could get along with three new dresses each, since we had just finished several before we got the invitation. However, we had only seven days to make our dresses after we decided to go. We found pretty much what we wanted in Davis's store. We bought a very pretty Dolly Varden each—mine had beautiful red roses on a black ground with a border to match and trimmings of the same on the three flounces which made the skirt. The dress had an infant waist with a broad sash to finish the costume, and I thought it quite a creation. Sister's had a black ground with morning glories of blue and pretty blue border made the same as mine. Then we each had a black cashmere with satin-brocaded flowers and black satin trimmings all shirred and puffed—a bustle overskirt all puffed out in the back—and ruffles galore. Our third dresses were wool—Sister's a light grey and mine a cream.

We had to make those six dresses in the few days we had left before Christmas, so we took the sewing machine down to the kitchen at the back of the house in order not to disturb the family. As soon as we got our patterns we started in, and when I think of it now I don't see how we ever finished those dresses—just sheer determination, I guess. We sat up every night until two or three o'clock and got them done just in time. Right pretty dresses they were, too.

On the day before Christmas we were "robed and ready," and Father had one of his men drive us to Devine where we boarded the train for Pearsall. Arriving at the Hearn Hotel before dinner, we unpacked and began dressing. At dinner we ran into a bunch of our friends from Friotown and in a very short time had escorts to the Christmas Eve ball, and from then on such a time as we had! Every night during the week there was a dance which always lasted until almost daylight, and we didn't feel that we could waste the time sleeping much during the day. The whole crowd was always gathered at the hotel, and there was fun going on all the time. We were so worn out when we got home, from sitting up sewing before Christmas and staying up during the holidays, that I think we slept most of several days. Sixty years later we still talk of the hilarious time we had that Christmas.

Our Christmas celebrations never ended with one day. We carried them on all during Christmas Week. Even yet we haven't abandoned the habit, but keep up the jollity and enjoyment from Christmas Eve until New Years. We had a good time for weeks beforehand, too, making doll furniture, dressing dolls, helping the neighbors with their doll clothes and with the arrangements for their Christmas enjoyments. We have a group of friends who have had Christmas together for the last ten years, each one having an eggnog party and dinner on a different day. By the time we have got around to all of them, we have run several days beyond New Years. Oh, how I love Christmas!

Another gala day was the Fourth of July, especially after the desperadoes and Indians had been driven out of our part of the country. Several days beforehand, our men folks began to build a platform for dancing, generally under those large oak trees at the Bramlette well where there was probably a quarter of an acre of shade. The platform was quite large—I suppose about seventy-five feet square—and was made by laying a floor of pine lumber over a foundation of four-by-sixes and building seats all around. The floor was waxed until it seemed as slick as glass. They put up swings, see-saws, and all kinds of things for the amusement of the children. Finally they dug a pit for barbecuing the beeves, pigs, and lambs that the people gave. On the night before the Fourth a couple of Negroes, experts at the barbecuing game, began to get the meat ready for the big festival, and early in the morning of the Great Day itself people began gathering with their cakes, pies, watermelons, cantaloupes, grapes, peaches and other kinds of fruit. The men had already ordered bread, pickles, ice cream, and everything else that could not be obtained in our near-by small towns from San Antonio. We had great tubs of pink lemonade and everything else good that one could think of. People came to the celebration from miles around—from Friotown, Pearsall, Devine, Pleasanton, Moore, and even from San Antonio, with Art's band bringing up the rear. Sometimes there were three hundred people.

We had a sixty or seventy-foot table made of planks. The ladies would spread their white tablecloths end to end and stack on all the good things. Everyone would take his plate to where the barbecue was being served at other long tables, and the feast would begin.

People looked forward to the Fourth of July with great anticipation from one year to the next, and no wonder, they enjoyed themselves so much. When everyone had feasted to his satisfaction, the band would begin playing and everybody danced, both young and old. How we loved those quadrilles! I'm sorry for anyone who has missed that thrill. Someone would call out the figures, singing at the same time, and oh joy! what a stampede. The eating and drinking and dancing went on all day and far into the next morning. Even people who had a long way to go next day had plenty to eat and plenty of coffee to drink before starting home.

Cleaning up the wreck next day was the bad feature, with all the women trying to get back the dishes, pans, tablecloths, and other belongings they had brought, while the men cleaned up the grounds and took the platform, tables, swings, and see-saws down. That wasn't so much fun, but everybody was happy over the good time they had had and were already looking forward to the next year when the same thing would be repeated.

HENRY AND THE WEDDING

W<small>E MET HENRY</small> on one of our trips to San Antonio. Dad and Uncle John Jordan frequently went there in our wagon to buy supplies at Stumberg's store for the home farm and ranch. In those days people had time to visit and be sociable, and there was always a lot of that sort of thing done on these trips. It was quite natural for them to become well acquainted with Henry Leuthy, a young man employed in the Stumberg store. They learned that he had always planned to go West and some time own a cattle ranch. His parents did not agree, but when he reached the age of twenty-one he took Horace Greeley's advice and, over their protest, headed west from his home in St. Joseph, Missouri. Young Henry was very much thrilled when the Stumbergs told him that they had two mighty good customers who lived on ranches and that he might be able to go out with them and look the ranching situation over. He was so thrilled he could hardly wait for these people to come, and when they finally did put in an appearance he broached the subject to them at once.

In those days there was an unwritten law in the West that no man took another's employee, so Dad said, "How about it, George? This young man thinks he wants to try ranching for a while."

George Stumberg replied, "Yes, I know, and I'll be glad for him to try it. If he doesn't like it, his place here is always open."

George told Father that Henry was one of the finest young men he had ever had in his employ, that he was always honest, industrious, and far-seeing, that Henry was cut out for better things than being a clerk in a grocery and dry goods store and he wouldn't stand in the way. Dad was delighted with the arrangement, so he brought Henry home with him. I have heard Mother say often that her heart went out to Henry the moment she saw him. He was a clean, tall, slender boy with long, easy-swinging arms and legs, a lean, kind face, a mop of unruly light hair, and deep blue eyes with a lot of understanding in them and a twinkle that always came at the right moment. He was quick to think but slow to express an opinion, always weighing matters before commenting on them. From the time he came to our house until Mother died, they were always great friends. Father too always thought a great deal of Henry and had every confidence in him.

He took to ranch life like a duck to water and learned about ranching and cattle so quickly and easily that it wasn't long before Dad took him in as a partner, and soon he was able to take over the running of the ranch.

Sister Alice and I were about seven or eight years of age when he came to live with the family. Every one of us loved him because he was as good as gold and as honest and straightforward as they ever make them.

The reason for all this detail about Henry is the fact that ten years after his twenty-first birthday we were busily engaged in preparing for his wedding, and the bride-to-be was my sister Alice who at that time was eighteen years old.

No one was more surprised than I to hear of it. When Sister told me that Henry was going to ask Mother's and Father's consent to their marriage, I was all full of curiosity to know how that was done and made up my mind to watch for an opportunity to overhear the conversation. One day, soon after Sister told me, I saw Dad coming up from the well and saw Henry start out to meet him. The corn crib was about half way between the well and the house, so I took off to the corn crib, going around the opposite way from the path that Henry was following. I rushed in behind the crib, peeked around the corner, and there I saw Dad stopping to talk with Henry and saying something about some cattle that had strayed away. Henry kept kicking up the corn cobs, first with one foot and then with the other. I would peek out for a while; then sneak back where I couldn't be seen and snicker to myself. Every time I peeked I could see that Henry was trying to get up courage to ask the great question, but Dad kept coming back to the lost stock. After pawing up about half an acre of dirt and sand and making half a dozen attempts, Henry finally said, "But Mr. Bramlette, what I'm trying to ask you is for your consent for Alice and I to be married."

Dad looked terribly surprised, and almost as embarrassed as Henry did. After quite a time he recovered himself enough to say, "Henry, Alice is too young to think about being married. If she were old enough I don't think I know anyone I'd sooner see her marry than you."

About that time I came out from my hiding place, laughing at their embarrassment and saying "Oh, my! that was fun!"

Father said, "What in the dickens are you doing out here?"

I said, "I just came out to hear Henry ask you to let him marry Alice."

I think they both would have liked to give me a frailing. Every time I came near Henry I'd start kicking up the dirt and saying, "But Mr. Bramlette. . . ." I teased him until I think he almost hated me, and I don't blame him much if he did. I never knew when he asked Mother, though I thought I was keeping a pretty good watch. I suppose I was out hunting some other kind of devilment to get into, for it seemed I was always into something. I think it was a great disappointment to the relatives that I didn't disgrace the family name, for they were always expecting it.

I think they thought their wishes were realized when I had been married for some time and decided I must have a divorce. When they found I was contemplating such a procedure they came from far and near—uncles, aunts, cousins, and all the family friends, I think, pleading with me not to think of such a thing. They admitted they didn't or couldn't blame me for separating from my husband, but there had never been a divorce in the family and they didn't want to see one now. They all put on a death-bed look when I said, "That being the case, I think it high time we were having one. I'm going to break the record." And the hard-headed Fan introduced the first divorce ever known in the family, though there have been others since. I often wonder if the divorcees that came after me would have gone forward with their plans if they had been pleaded with as I was.

But to get back to the wedding. After Henry had gained the consent of both parents, he began saying he couldn't see any reason for delaying the happy event. The time was finally set for the first of May, that being his thirty-first birthday, and the preparations were begun.

We had about a month to prepare. Sister's trousseau was to be made, since there was no place at that time where we could buy ready-made things. Sister and I being handy with the sewing machine, we got out our embroidery, laces, beadings, and ribbons and it didn't take us long to finish the lingerie, though she had eight suits of everything.

Then came the making of the wedding dress and the "second day" dress. The wedding dress was very pretty, made of a soft cream wool combined with cream satin—no train—which she wore with a wreath of orange blossoms and a short veil. We worked for days and part of the nights on those dresses before we finally got them finished.

Then began the house cleaning. The parts which we didn't do ourselves we had to oversee, and it was quite a task. After the cleaning came the cooking; and such a lot of cakes, pies, bread, salads, boiled and baked hams, chickens, turkeys, and beef roasts, I never saw before, and at that we didn't have any too much, for people came from far and near—from Friotown, from Cotulla, from Pearsall, from Pleasanton, from Moore, not to mention the gentry from the immediate neighborhood.

The men folks, Henry, Father, and Uncle Sam Thomas, who with his family was there helping us, put up a long table in the back yard where a hundred people or more could eat at one time. Even this couldn't accommodate all the people so we set out small tables in order that all might be served. On either side of the table they put up posts on which to hang lanterns for light. Lanterns were the only kind of light that wouldn't blow out when put outdoors. We had twenty lanterns, using what we had and borrowing the rest from the neighbors.

As the time drew near for the wedding I decided I had to have a new dress made for the affair, for wasn't Dave Little coming from Friotown, and didn't I too want to look my best? I chose a pink nunsveiling and was quite pleased with myself when the time came to wear it. I was not in such a pleasant frame of mind otherwise, since Henry had had Bill Ballon visiting him—a friend from San Antonio—and I had halfway promised to marry him. I was afraid both boys would be at the wedding, which would put me in somewhat of a dilemma.

The morning of the day arrived—all of us in a flutter—everybody up early and at it. The house must be decorated; the long table in the yard prettied up with white table cloths, centerpieces, and flowers; the food all got ready. All the food that could be prepared the day before was ready, but there were many things that couldn't be prepared in advance, and we were glad that we had several relatives assisting. I remember that we had two of those long stove boilers which held about five gallons each filled with coffee and put on to boil, and as soon as one was empty it would be filled up again. I suppose at least forty gallons of coffee were consumed before the day was over.

By seven o'clock we had taken everything out of the large front room so as to have space for the dancers. At that time nothing was complete if there was no dancing attached. There were seats around everywhere. Our large front porch was filled with them and so was the front yard. This left the front room entirely bare except for the place arranged for the musicians to sit and for the decorations in front of the fireplace. We had banked it with greenery and put large pots of flowers on either side. The bride and groom were to stand there facing the audience and the preacher.

People started arriving as early as five o'clock. Some of

them had to come a long way, and of course couldn't count on arriving at any fixed time. Some of the family were ready to receive them as they came, there being eight or ten near relatives who had come earlier, a few the day before. The ceremony was to be at eight o'clock, and before that time it looked as if a hundred and fifty people were there. Hacks, wagons, buggies, and horses were all around the yard fence and fifty yards out from it. The lanterns in the yard were all lighted, the house brilliantly lit up, and everything looking very festive. We were all ready except for the preacher. He had some trouble getting across the creek near Devine as there had been heavy rains up above and he had to wait until the water ran down before he could cross. We began to get nervous for fear he couldn't make it, but about eight-thirty he drove in and we called the young couple to come out—the preacher had arrived.

Sister came out in all her bridal finery looking "mighty like a rose"—prettier, I think, than I ever saw her, though she had the reputation of being the prettiest girl in the neighborhood. Also out came Henry in his black broadcloth suit, looking like Prince Albert or somebody equally distinguished. Standing by the improvised altar, they were married in a very short ceremony by Brother Hukill of the Devine Baptist Church.

After the marriage, everyone was invited out to the table and given a sumptuous wedding supper. Six or seven of the family served them from the kitchen, and they all ate to their fullest satisfaction.

After supper the music started and dancing began, lasting until sunup the next morning. Then breakfast was served for those who had come from far away. The bride and groom took an early morning train for San Antonio, where they spent their honeymoon.

Are you wondering if Dave came? He did. And we were both very happy. He stayed until after breakfast next morning and then left for his thirty-five-mile horseback ride home.

IN BUSINESS

THE LAXSONS, OUR OLD-TIME FRIENDS, came from Cotulla for the wedding, and when it was over they invited me to go home with them for a visit. Needless to say I was up and ready, and with Mother's consent I left with them the morning after the wedding.

I had a wonderful time on that visit. They gave a party for me so that I could meet the young folks. I am not bragging, I hope, but in those days I always had all the beaus I needed to take me wherever I wished to go. Cotulla was no exception. I met several nice young men there while visiting with my friends—two or three with whom I kept up a correspondence for a long time after my return home.

Back in the country again, things seemed very dull, and I began looking around for some place to go. I loved people, and lots of them, and everything at home soon settled down into such a routine that I began to get restless. When Mother noticed that I was bored, she would ask me to go out to the garden with her (she and Cap Wallace always made a lovely garden). She would show me what nice beans they had growing and would say, "Look how Mr. Wallace's young corn is making silks." I would think, "Now I wonder if she is going to drag me clear across the garden to look at that old corn"— so bored I could hardly stand it.

I wanted to go where I could see other things besides the farm and ranch—where things were going on. It seemed the only pleasure I had was to mount my beautiful Black Bess and gallop over the hills. Sister wasn't much fun, now that she was married. She thought she had to act "old-marriedy." I was quite put to it to find something to do.

While I was so downcast, I happened to see an advertisement in the Pearsall *News*. Miss Ida Staley, the town milliner and dressmaker, was advertising for an apprentice, someone to learn the milliner and dress-making trade. I read the advertisement and I thought, "Now if I can only manage some way to get there without letting Mother and Dad know about it, I'm surely going to try my luck." Just to think! I could live in town where I had always wanted to live. Besides, I thought, I'd just love to learn to make hats and improve myself in dressmaking. The longer I thought about the plan, the more determined I became to try it out. So I wrote Miss Staley telling her I should like the place, and telling her also who I was and who my relatives were in Pearsall. A letter came right back replying that she would hold the place open for me if I could get there within the coming week. That was one time I lost sleep planning how to get away. I knew Father would never consent, for he had often remarked that he never wanted any of his children to engage in any kind of work and didn't think they would have to. But Dad was in Houston, where he had shipped a car load of hogs to market. And now if I could only get Mother away for the day I might manage it. But how to do that! I couldn't think of a way until one of Uncle John Thomas's boys (Marion, I think it was) came over in their gig. I got him off where I could talk to him and promised him a dollar if he would tell Mother that he had come for her—that Aunt Sarah wanted her to come over and spend the day. Marion was much younger than I and a dollar looked pretty big to a kid in those days. Marion approached Mother immediately.

She started making excuses, saying she couldn't see how she was going to get away that day—the wash woman was coming, and she had to do a lot of other things. I was shaking in my shoes and thinking, "Oh, Lord! I wonder if she is not going." I added my entreaties to Marion's telling her it would be a shame after Aunt Sarah had sent all the way over for her if she didn't go, and perhaps it was something important. Sister

Alice, I said, could see to the wash woman now that she was so grown up, and anyway since she was married she had better be learning something about housekeeping; she wasn't a bit of fun any more, anyway.

When finally Mother consented to go, I commenced tearing around trying to rush her off in time for me to get to Devine to catch a two-o'clock train for Pearsall. I had been getting things ready and packing my trunk ever since I had got the letter from Miss Staley. All I had to do was lock it and get into my town clothes. It was eleven o'clock before she left. I had to call the Mexican man who drove the hack and get him to harness the horses. This would take some little time, so I simply flew out to where the man was plowing. I told him to hurry to the house and hitch up the hack—that I had to get to Devine at once. He came, but he meandered in as if he had all the rest of his life to get there.

I kept saying, "*Andale, andale!*" but he kept on at the same speed. When he reached the house he announced that he must get another team—he couldn't use the one he had been plowing with. I was frantic. "No," I screamed at him. "Use those horses. And hurry—hurry!"

About this time Sister Alice came out and wanted to know what on earth I was doing. I said, "If you want to know, I'm going to Pearsall to work in a millinery store." She was shocked, of course, that I hadn't told her anything about it. I always had told her everything, but she had been acting so superior since she was a married woman—just as if I couldn't have been married two or three times if I had wanted to.

She laughed when I said I was going to work in a millinery store and said right sarcastically, "I'd just love to wear a hat you'd make."

I knew she would not have hesitated to let Mother know of my plans if she had had an opportunity. She really wanted me at home for company when her newly acquired husband wasn't there. But I knew she had no way of communicating with Mother and felt very secure about telling her.

After I had scolded for what seemed like an hour, the pokey old Mexican finally got the horses hitched up and ready to start. Then came the problem of getting my heavy old trunk into the back of the hack, he declaring it was too heavy for him to lift in alone and insisting on going out to the field a couple of hundred yards away to get somebody to help him. Knowing that it would take him forever and seeing that he wouldn't lift the trunk in himself, I said, "*Bueno*, I'll go get Juan myself."

I tore off down to the field, thinking, "I'll take a near cut, climb over the fence, and make it much quicker." But as I was getting over the fence I made a misstep and literally tore my dress off me. By this time, with all my hurrying and scurrying to make that train, I was in a terrible state and just gave way. I started bawling as loud as I could, and Juan, hearing me, thought something dreadful had happened and started running towards me at top speed, leaving his team without even stopping them. About the time he reached me, I looked up and saw horses, plow, and everything, streaking across the field with the sand and dust just flying. I thought, "My Lord! What have I done now?"—for I knew the team would be simply cut to pieces with the plow.

Fortunately, just when I had almost given up, the horses ran astride a pole that was sticking up in the field, and that stopped them. Another of the field hands happened to be coming across the field and he ran to them, unhitched them from the plow, and led them in only slightly the worse for wear. A few small cuts were bleeding quite profusely, but none of them were serious.

I was sure by now that my trip would be in vain—that I would never catch that train. Anyway we got the trunk loaded on, after which I got into the hack and started urging the Mexican on at every step. We got there just in the nick of time as the old train was puffing into the depot. I certainly wasted no time rushing in and calling for my ticket. The trunk didn't get on, but when I got to Pearsall I related my predicament to the agent there, who was a family friend. He wired to Devine, and the trunk came in next day.

As luck would have it, when I got off the train at Pearsall I ran into one of my Aunt Mary Thomas's brothers who was there with his carriage, and I had no trouble getting to my Uncle Sam's house. He was the one who had lived with us so many years before his marriage—I really believe, one of the best men in the world. I wasn't the least bit afraid to tell him about my escapade. He too knew that if I had asked permission of my Mother and Father they would never have consented to my coming, and I think I must have had it in the back of my mind all the time that if I could just get to him he would fix everything all right with my parents.

From the time I was a small child I'd always wanted to do something for myself. When I was little, I would see the girls clerking in the stores in San Anonio, all dressed up and looking so pretty and attractive, and I would think, "How I would love to do that." But in those days, particularly among Southern people, girls never thought of working. Even the school teachers were looked at askance. Uncle Sam saw it my way, however, and the very day I arrived he wrote to Mother telling her to leave me alone and let me try it out. He felt sure I would get tired and give it up soon. I also wrote Mother begging to stay. It was some time before I heard from her, and meanwhile there was the job waiting.

In the morning Aunt Mary helped me to get all dressed up and Uncle Sam drove me down in the carriage as he went to his office (Uncle Sam was district clerk at this time). He took me in and introduced me to Miss Staley, and told her if I got too troublesome to send me to him. I was so delighted I hardly knew what to do. There were so many beautiful hats and other pretty things. It was wonderful to go to work at Miss Staley's. For a long time Uncle Sam would drive by each evening and take me to his house, but finally Miss Staley decided she wanted me to stay with her since at that time she was fitting two wealthy young ladies out with their trousseaus. One of them, such a beautiful woman, was a relative of the Blockers and lived on their ranch. She was to be married to a man from Houston. I noticed that she was a much older girl than my sister Alice and I wondered why Sister hadn't waited until she was grown up like this lovely lady.

She had some of the most beautiful dresses I had ever seen. One that I still remember vividly was a brown broadcloth made with a redingote. It was beautifully made, Miss Staley being a real modiste, and it fitted her beautiful form to perfection. She chose to wear it with a lovely brown velvet hat which was ornamented with three gorgeous plumes fastened on with a knot of silk plush and a bronze buckle. With this costume she wore brown shoes and carried a brown bag. Another of the dresses we made for her was a maroon cashmere which had a pointed basque with innumerable buttons down the front and a draped skirt. There was also a dark blue dress, and then came the dress of dresses, a magnificent Skinner's satin made in princess style with a deep collar of rare old lace which had been in the family for years. The train had gores of lace set in, and was very long. The dress was made with a square neck and with sleeves which came to the hand.

We worked busily on this trousseau. The girl was very much worried for fear we couldn't get it finished, and I felt quite elated when Miss Staley said that if she hadn't had such excellent help she couldn't have got it done in time.

I don't seem to remember much about the other young girl whose trousseau we made, but I know there were a lot of nice things to be turned out and it took some time to finish them. It seems strange that some people have such personalities that you can remember even their little mannerisms while others whom you meet at the same time and just as often make little impression and you can't remember one thing about them. It was that way in the case of these two girls. I shall always remember the girl of the brown broadcloth dress, with her beautiful blue eyes, brown wavy hair, and dimpled cheeks, while the other one I can't remember one thing about.

I loved my stay in Pearsall and perhaps would have lingered there indefinitely but for something that came up unexpectedly. After I had been there for several months we heard that there was some kind of a boom at Brownsville. At least a friend of Miss Staley's kept writing her letters about how well she could do there with her business, and after thinking about it for some time she decided to move everything to Brownsville. She wanted me to go there with her, but I thought I had strayed far enough away from the family fold already and wrote the folks I was coming home.

I helped Miss Staley all I could with her packing and getting ready for her new home. I bought hats (which Miss Staley assisted me in trimming) for my three sisters. Then I packed my trunk and took my way back to the rancho. The hat I bought for sister Alice was a lovely blue horsehair braid trimmed with three blue plumes of the same color. When she put it on she was so entranced with it I couldn't help saying, "And I thought you remarked you'd like to wear a hat that I trimmed."

"You overdid yourself on this," she replied. "I didn't think you had it in you."

Lourene Cochran, Aunt Fan's daughter, age seven (Frances Bramlette Farris Collection).

A HOME OF MY OWN

THERE I WAS BACK ON THE RANCH again with nothing to do. I must admit, however, that we had some excitement occasionally. While I was away Sister and Henry had moved into a house several hundred yards from where Father and Mother lived, so Mother and the two small girls and I were often alone and we never felt quite safe at night. Always we kept something of a lookout for the Mexicans who made raids in the surrounding country, robbing houses, driving off horses, and doing quite a lot of mischief.

We had a big, unruly, half-crazy Mexican on the ranch whom we were afraid of because he acted so queer when the men called him to the house to attend to anything they wanted done. One night we were alone—Mother, my sisters Virginia and Effie, and I. Old Jesus, the half-crazy Mexican, kept lingering around the house after he had got the wood in for the morning fires. He wanted to know when the *mestro* would be home. Of course we didn't tell him that we were not expecting Father home that night. Finally Mother asked him what he wanted and why he didn't go home. He said he was waiting for the *mestro*. Mother told him to go on home and come back in the morning. He lingered a while, then sidled off, looking back all the time.

Mother said, "That old Mexican is up to something," and told us we had better not sleep too soundly since it was after dark when he left. She decided we had better all sleep in one room, so we managed to get two beds fixed up in the front bedroom that looked out on the front porch. Mother got the old shotgun down and loaded it, and then we all lay down for a night's vigil. None of us dared to think of sleep. It was a moonlight night, and some time after midnight we saw a black form creeping up to the front porch. It was Jesus. He sat down on the edge of the porch, pulled a long-bladed knife out of the front of his shirt, and began whetting it on a whet rock he had brought with him. He would sit and whet a while, then stand up and laugh—the most maniacal laughter I ever heard out of any human being—at the same time waving his arms around over his head. Then he'd sit down and sharpen his knife some more. He kept that up for what seemed like hours, and all the while Mother was standing just inside the front door with the shotgun leveled on him. Had he attempted to come into the house, she was ready for him; but he kept waving his knife and shrieking until my brother-in-law, hearing the noise from where he lived, jumped out of bed and came tearing up to the house. He ran up to the front, where Jesus was cutting up his didoes, and when Jesus saw him he took to his heels. Henry grabbed the shotgun and fired it in the direction Jesus had gone, but he was too far away for the shots to do him any harm.

Next day the crazy old wretch came up, all smiles, and howdy-does, wanting to know if we were scared. He said he was waiting for the *mestro* to come home and was just playing to keep from going to sleep. I suppose he made the men believe it, for they kept him on for several years, but we were always wary of him. I really think he knew there were no men on the place and thought he could scare us out of the house so he could rob it of what things he wanted. He probably imagined there was money in the house, for all the peons thought the white folks were very wealthy.

As soon as we calmed down after that episode, I began to be restless again. To pass the time I often went to visit the Cochran family, who were still living in the settlement in one of Father's houses. I was very fond of the two girls, Laura and Queen, and also of their two brothers Jim and M. B. The latter, M. B., was very jolly and full of fun and went places with us girls when there was any place to go. For a wonder Mother didn't object to our being with them. They were good, honest, hard-working people and she could find no excuse to keep us from going with them until one of the sons who had never been there appeared on the scene—a dashing young man, quite good-looking, who had a way with the girls. He seemed to take quite an interest in me from the start, and I liked him.

It was some time before either of our families had any idea of our intentions, but when they did get onto it, there was some hades raised. My family thought there was nobody good enough for us girls to marry, and when his mother found that my mother and father were so terribly opposed to my marrying Dick, she too took an arbitrary stand, saying that those Bramlette girls knew nothing about work and did nothing but dress up and sit around and read. If he married one of them, he would have a hard row to hoe. All of which made us more determined than ever. In a short time we slipped off, got our license, and were married.

Shortly after this happened, Father and Mother decided to give each of us girls a small ranch of our own. Mine was located where the old Laxson place had stood just across the Bigfoot-Devine road from the rocky hill on which my father's home was built. Each of these places had only 320 acres, but this was enough to make a very good-sized farm with land left over for a number of cattle. We lived there until both our children had grown to school age.

My son Ewell came along without any trouble, but in June of 1889, when we were awaiting the arrival of his sister, things did not go so smoothly. My brother-in-law Jim Cochran and his wife, who lived in the same locality, were also expecting, and we had sent for my mother-in-law to come and officiate at both occasions for we thought we could never pull through an illness or have a baby without her. She came from her home in Wimberly, Hays County, where she had recently moved, and assisted at the arrival of Jim's little daughter Edna, but my child was delayed longer than Mrs. Cochran felt she could stay away from her other patients. So I packed up and went with her, making the trip from Bigfoot to Wimberly in a hack. A week later my little daughter was born. We named her Isabelle Lourene for my mother, my mother-in-law, and a friend, Aunt Rena Mayo, who assisted at her arrival. We thought we had given her a very nice name. We took her home on the train when she was three weeks old—such a small, yellow, sickly-looking child that when one of my sisters saw her she said, "She is so ugly I can't like her much." My father, however, was interested in her from the beginning, and it didn't take long for her to single him out as her special ally. The friendship lasted as long as he lived. She was always his companion, and when he lay ill so long, she went from El Paso, where we were living, to Bigfoot to help nurse him through his last sickness though she was only seventeen years old at the time.

The question of her name has never been entirely settled. When friends began coming in to see the new baby they would say, "Isn't she a cute little trick?" until her brother Ewell began calling her Trick and then Trixie. To this day most of our friends call her Trixie, and though some few call her Lorene none of them ever use her real name, Lourene.

She was very ill for a long time and many times we thought she would not live. Finally she got better, but she was never strong and consequently did not join the other children in strenuous play, preferring the companionship of older people.

In those days children were supposed to be seen but not heard, but she was always very much in evidence, listening to all that was said and then asking questions. This irked my mother, who would say, "She is entirely too forward for a child of her age and had better be stopped." Dad would answer, "Leave her alone. She knows what she's doing."

I remember one of her little outbursts that shocked me, though I couldn't help being amused. It was when she was older and had been staying with the Holcombes in Devine. She was coming home for a few days and I worked to get things in order and have the house as attractive as possible in honor of her homecoming. I took special pride in the table— had put a pretty cloth on it with some new napkins I had made to match, had arranged what I thought was a pretty centerpiece of flowers, and had cooked her favorite food. Ewell seemed to resent all the attention she was getting, and we had no sooner sat down at the table than he started teasing her. She deliberately took the plate of biscuits and threw them at him, one at a time, until they were all gone. And so the homecoming didn't end as pleasantly as I had planned it.

I told her I was surprised and shocked at her behavior and had had an idea that she would at least learn some manners at school. Cap Wallace spoke up and said, "What did you expect? Did you think she would come home with flowing curls, rosy cheeks, and pearly teeth?" It seemed with Cap Wallace and Father around she always had a champion.

They were not her only friends. We always had a great many Mexican families on the two ranches in whom both the children were much interested. They learned to speak Spanish almost before they learned English, quizzed their Mexican friends about their religion and legends, and learned a great deal about their way of life. I can still see Mother setting forth on a dark night, Trixie leading the way with a lantern, to help some poor Mexican who was snake-bitten or suddenly taken ill. Her association with the Mexicans was helpful to her in after years for she got into social work through her knowledge of Spanish. When the big flood washed most of East El Paso away, the Red Cross asked her to help in the rehabilitation. A short time later there was a call for volunteers to go to Illinois, where there was another flood disaster, and after her return she went to work for the El Paso County Welfare Board. Eventually she became its secretary and kept the place until her health broke in 1939, when she came out to San Diego to join her husband, her daughter, and me.

During Trixie's childhood it seemed that her father was away from home most of the time. He was a jolly, big-hearted, restless fellow who wouldn't stay put. He bought, sold, and traded ranches, horses, cattle, and anything else that would keep him on the go. He was constantly on the verge of a big deal that would set us up for life, and sometimes had such rosy hopes of a fortune right in the offing that I'd pack up the children, join him, and stay till the bubble burst. Then

back again to the ranch we would have to go. He always said,
"Now don't worry. I'll soon be home with so much money
that there will never be another occasion for anyone to be
disturbed." And that went on through many years. Our last
venture was at Eagle Lake, where there was a sure fortune.
We stayed there a while and the fortune didn't materialize;
then he took our young son and struck out for Houston,
where it was surely to be found this time, leaving Trixie and
me at Eagle Lake, where she developed malarial fever. Then
for the first and only time in my life I had to ask Father to send
for us. Up to that time I'd always managed some way at the
end of one of these ventures to get back to the ranch. I was so
afraid of that "I told you so" that I never wanted to let them
know when we weren't getting on so well. It couldn't be
helped this time, however, and when my husband finally appeared on the scene three months later, Dad laid down the law
and said that the children and I had taken our last trip without
proof that we were going to a place at least as good as the one
we were leaving. He said it had to stop because the children's
lives up to that time had been spent on the way between the
ranch and some place where there was a million dollars.

By the time the children had grown to school age I began
to feel that it was my turn to leave. It was such a long way to
the nearest school (at Bigfoot) that it was decided I should go
to Devine with the children. There happened to be a millinery
store in Devine which was for sale at the time. I felt that I
could do the establishment justice, and we decided to buy it.
So we moved there, leaving my husband, Bigfoot Wallace,
and Little Joe McInerny to keep house on the farm. Little Joe
was an Irishman my husband had picked up who had no
home and was delighted to get some place to stay. He was a
good cook, did the housework, and attended to the chickens.
He was such a success in the chicken business that he brought
several cages of eggs to town to sell every week, for which he
got all the money himself.

It was in Devine that I first met Colonel George Holcombe and Mrs. Holcombe, and we became fast friends, a
friendship which continued for many years. My millinery ad-

venture lasted for two years and I was quite successful, but the men at home got restless and I thought things would go along better if I were there, so I sold out my business to Mrs. Holcombe, she taking charge of the youngsters' schooling as well as the business. Those dear good friends kept the children for three years after I went to the ranch, and the youngsters loved them almost as much as they did their own parents.

The Holcombes and the children spent most of the weekends with us. It was on one of these visits that Colonel Holcombe decided to go to Aransas Pass to look after the claim which Bigfoot Wallace gave to me and made a very successful sale of the property. Immediately we began building a new house on the ranch, where Mr. Wallace lived with us until his death. It seemed that the workmen were forever getting the house finished, so eager was I to get into it; but finally the last nail was driven and it didn't take long to get moved and settled. Though it wasn't very grand or pretentious, I was very happy there and loved my new house. Both the children loved living there and could hardly wait for Friday night to come, when someone would go into Devine to bring them home for the weekend, generally accompanied by Colonel and Mrs. Holcombe.

We hadn't been in our new home very long when A. J. Sowell came to see Bigfoot Wallace about writing a sketch of his life. His daughter Media came with him. They stayed several days, and when they left it was with the understanding that Mr. Sowell would return shortly and begin his *Life of Bigfoot Wallace*. Knowing he would be with us for some time, I began preparing to make his stay as pleasant as possible. In those days, unlike today, every person didn't require a separate room, so I moved an extra bed into Mr. Wallace's room and the two of them occupied it together. Often they talked and visited until very late. Jack Sowell was a very pleasant person and it wasn't long until he became almost one of the family. The first time he came to see us he found out through Mr. Wallace how very fond I was of pets, so when he returned he brought me the cutest little squirrel. The little fellow

seemed to fit right into the family and never showed any in-
clination to run away, so we just turned him loose in the
house. He ran all over the place and I would often find him
coiled up beside me in the bed at night.

He liked milk and cream, and after he got up to a good
size would climb anywhere to get them. I had a box fixed up
for my milk on the back porch and kept a white piece of
sheeting gathered and inserted in the vessel. This allowed the
water to soak through and drip over the milk to keep it cool.
On several occasions when I got up in the morning I would
find the cheesecloth unfastened and every particle of cream
skimmed off the milk. I accused the men, who always had the
run of the house, everyone feeling so much at home that
whenever anyone felt like a cup of coffee he was at perfect
liberty to go into the kitchen and help himself. I usually kept a
pot of coffee on the stove, and if there was none made and the
men felt like making it, they were free to do so. So I called in
the bunch—Cap Wallace, Jack Sowell, Uncle Joe, and my
husband—and told them all to stop leaving my milk box
open and to quit skimming all the cream off for their coffee.
They couldn't possibly use all that cream. All declared their
innocence; so one morning I got up earlier than usual to investigate, and there was Jack the squirrel (I had named him for
Jack Sowell, who gave him to me). He had pulled the cheesecloth up and was inside the box waving his bushy tail across
the milk pans. I stood still to see what he was going to do, and
do you know, when he had got all the cream on his tail that it
would hold, he hopped up on top of the milk box and licked
it all off. I still watched, and lo and behold he went through
the same maneuver the second time.

I thought, "Young man, that's just adding insult to injury," and I took him and put him in his cage—kept him there
for several days. He was never so cute and friendly after that,
but started going away and staying a day or two at a time.
Finally he went away and never came back. I was very sad
over losing him and wondered if some boy out hunting had
killed the dear little creature. We all searched for him, but to
no avail.

BY AND BY HARD TIMES

Times were getting pretty hard in Frio County and in
all the country where there were large herds and big ranches.
One reason was the fact that our great expanses of vacant
territory attracted farmers and small ranchers who drove in
their own herds and interfered with the large cattle outfits.
Another reason was a drouth which lasted several years. Between the two the cattle business was almost out of commis-
sion, especially in our community. Father and my brother-in-
law Henry had put in large fields of cotton and corn which
really paid quite well for some time, but that was finished too
when the boll weevils came in and started devastating the cotton crops. We fought them for some time, but Henry finally
gave up when a brother in El Paso wrote him that he could
get him a good position if he would sell out his interests in
Frio County and come out there. So he sold what cattle he
had left, and he and Sister Canby Alice left for El Paso. It was
a great shock to the family, for we all lived in such close prox-
imity through the years braving the dangers of Comanches,
Mexicans, and outlaws. I know it was the best thing for them
to do; in fact, the rest of us later followed their example.

It was not long after Captain Wallace's death that we began to think about it. Colonel Holcombe had printed Jack
Sowell's book and we had folded and prepared it for binding
in my home. The Colonel himself was about to move away.
And so one day the family got together and held a conclave.
There seemed nothing much left to stay for in Frio County,
and we wanted to make up our minds what to do and where
to go. It was finally decided that Dad would go ahead and

investigate several places where we had heard that living was easier. We had been hearing especially about the Mesilla Valley in New Mexico—how the fruit, vegetables, and everything a person might want to plant grew and produced there. Father had visions of buying up large tracts and cutting them up into small farms so as to sell them at a big profit, or else buying and stocking a cattle ranch somewhere in New Mexico.

We had a neighbor boy of whom Dad was very fond— young Charley Grumbles, a son of Ed Grumbles who was murdered with Mack Kercheville by bandits. Dad called Charley in one day after we had grown enthusiastic and excited about moving to New Mexico, and said, "Charley, how would you like to take a long trip? I'd like you to go with me to hunt a better land."

Charley was right in for it.

Dad said, "Now we don't want to travel on the train, for we want to stop at many places and look over the country." That seemed reasonable, so Dad took the covered spring hack, lengthened the bed, attached a provision box to the back, took his army cot and set it inside with mattress and covers, and said to Charley, "I can drive while you are lying down, and you can drive while I am lying down." And that was how Dad took his first Pullman ride. They started out with Charley's canvas cot folded up and Dad's set up ready for occupancy at a moment's notice. Dad loved his siesta—had acquired the habit, I think, even before he came to live near the border on the other side of which the natives close up their businesses for a couple or three hours in the middle of the day.

After they had repainted the hack, loaded their bedding, and provisioned their outfit, we all went out to watch the take-off, and though they looked somewhat comical starting off on that long journey of a thousand miles or more, we couldn't help admiring the roomy and comfortable appearance of their home-made Pullman.

In the words of the old Negro song, they were "starting out to hunt a happy land." Those of us who were left behind got a world of thrills talking about the trip and planning what we were going to do when we got to our new world. Eagerly we watched for letters and cards telling us where they were and how fast they were travelling (which of necessity wasn't very fast). As they progressed, we planned our house . . . what kind of furniture we were going to have in it . . . how large the living room was going to be (it was to be very large) . . . how many bedrooms we were going to have . . . and a thousand other things which kept us supplied with topics for conversation.

Dad and Charley were gone for a long time. It seemed like an eternity before they finally came home, but at last there they were and we could hardly wait to get them inside the door before the questions began: "Have you found the place you wanted? Where is it? How does it look? Is there plenty of water? What does it grow?"—and so on. To all of which we got encouraging answers.

The next thing to do was to find a buyer or buyers for our land and to make our plans for getting away. The children, Trixie and Ewell, were very reluctant to leave their little Mexican playmates and wanted to know if the parents of little Jesus, little Juan, and little Maria couldn't go with us and work there for us the same as here. They loved playing with the little Mexicans, mostly, I think, because they could boss them, but also because they loved eating at the Mexican *jacales* where they would be given frijoles, enchiladas, and all the rest of their garlic-perfumed viands. Father promised to take all that wanted to go, but poor Father was destined never to go to the beautiful country he had found where apples, prunes, and peaches sometimes lay on the ground six inches thick and where a beautiful stream ran right through the ground he had managed to purchase. A few weeks after his return he was stricken with partial paralysis and lingered in that condition for several years before he died.

So our hopes of moving to a new home were blasted and it was a long time before we left the old place near Bigfoot. Mother lived there until her death. My daughter married Lee Massey there. I myself went to live in El Paso, where my sister and my children had made their homes, and there I married again.

We were farmers in the Rio Grande Valley north of El Paso. Life was pleasant there, though our terror of the dreaded Villistas was every bit as great as our earlier fear of the Comanches. Alone again, I joined my daughter and granddaughter in San Diego.

This is the end of the trail for me. It is lovely here. The climate is delightful. The flowers are so beautiful at all seasons; there are so many interesting places to go; so many interesting people to know. I think it is a great privilege to be allowed to live amidst such beauty and among so many wonderful friends.

I often think how different my life today is from the one I lived in the Indian country so many years ago. It is like thinking of two different worlds. In those days we had so little and now we have so much. For one thing we enjoy so much more companionship and friendship now than we could possibly have had on a Texas ranch in frontier times, and I do think our friends here are the most interesting anyone could have.

And yet my heart turns back sometimes to a frame house in the country south of San Antonio with a log kitchen out behind and a bright moon shining down on a happy family of children begging Captain Wallace for another story before bedtime. I don't think I ever want to go back there. They tell me the country has gone to rack and ruin—nothing left but worn-out fields and tumbledown houses. I should be sad to see the houses where we once lived so happily all gone to decay. I prefer to remember it as it was—the places where we children once played, swinging on the grape vines, riding wild steers, swimming in the branches, always on the lookout for Indians . . . the evenings we sat around listening to Uncle Wynn, Uncle Sam, Uncle John and Father arguing about Darwin's theory, Ingersoll, Tom Paine, and many other things our young minds could not digest . . . Bigfoot Wallace cooling his feet under the arbor at the back of the house . . . poor old Uncle Joe telling how his wife Mary got burned to death; taking down her enlarged picture from his bedroom wall and saying, "Come down here, Mary, you old wretch. You were worth every darn cent I ever spent on you" . . . the broad prairies waving in the wind like huge fields of wheat . . . the long-horned Texas cattle roving in their enormous pastures through grass half as high as they themselves were.

Some time ago I read an article in the *Southwest Review* in which J. Frank Dobie wrote of his longing for his Texas soil when he was in a foreign country; and another in which Sam Rayburn told of his love for his Texas home near Bonham. I can understand their feelings, but they still have homes to go back to while mine has been practically destroyed by drouth and the boll weevil. For me it is better just to remember.

Aunt Fan in her San Diego garden (Frances Bramlette Farris Collection).

Typesetting, in Bembo 11/13, by *G & S*, Austin
Printing, on 60 lb. Warren's Olde Style White, by
Edwards Brothers, Ann Arbor
Binding by *Edwards Brothers*
Woodcut by *Barbara Whitehead*
Design by Whitehead & Whitehead, Austin